THE
WHAT WOULD
JESUS EAT?
COOKBOOK

The
WHAT WOULD
JESUS
EAT?
COOKBOOK

DON COLBERT, M.D.

THOMAS NELSON
Since 1798

NASHVILLE DALLAS MEXICO CITY RIO DE JANEIRO

This book is not intended to provide medical advice or to take the place of medical advice and treatment from your personal physician. Readers are advised to consult their own doctors or other qualified health professionals regarding the treatment of their medical problems. Neither the publisher nor the author takes any responsibility for any possible consequences from any treatment, actions, or application of medicine, supplement, herb, or preparation to any person reading or following the information in this book. If readers are taking prescription medications, they should consult with their physicians and not take themselves off of medicines to start supplementation without the proper supervision of a physician. An exhaustive search was done to determine whether previously required permission to reprint. If there has been an error, please contact the publisher, and a correction will be made in subsequent editions.

Published in Nashville, Tennessee, by Thomas Nelson. Thomas Nelson is a registered trademark of Thomas Nelson, Inc.

Thomas Nelson, Inc. books may be purchased in bulk for educational, business, fund-raising, or sales promotional use. For information, please e-mail SpecialMarkets@ThomasNelson.com.

Scripture taken from the New King James Version®. Copyright © 1982 by Thomas Nelson, Inc. Used by permission. All rights reserved.

ISBN 978-0-7852-9842-7 (trade paper)

Library of Congress Cataloging-in-Publication Data
Colbert, Don.
   The what would Jesus eat? cookbook / Don Colbert.
      p. cm.
   Includes index.
   ISBN 978-0-7852-6519-1
   1. Cookery. 2. Cookery—Religious aspects. I. Title.
   TX715.C5733 2002
   641.5—dc21

                          2002007203

Printed in the United States of America
08 09 10 11 12 Edward's Brothers 14 13 12 11 10

CONTENTS

INTRODUCTION

IF YOU ARE THE AVERAGE AMERICAN, you are living your life in the fast lane, rarely taking time to relax, wind down, and enjoy a meal. Rather than making dining a pleasant experience, you may wolf your food down as you drive or as you sit in front of the TV. And you probably wash your meal down with a soft drink or sweetened tea.

Instead of eating in a rushed, stressed, and pressured manner, try eating the way Jesus ate, in a relaxed, peaceful atmosphere, surrounded with friends, laughing, conversing, and enjoying life—but always start by blessing the food. This is not only biblical; it also helps to relax our minds and bodies in preparation for receiving the food.

Breakfast in particular is becoming a lost tradition. For years, I have told patients to eat breakfast like a king, lunch like a prince, and dinner like a pauper. I strongly recommend that you never skip breakfast, since this is, by far, the most important meal of the day. Breakfast means simply "breaking the fast," which in turn will help keep the metabolic rate elevated, thus helping to prevent obesity. However, many people skip breakfast entirely and then eat a very small lunch and a very large dinner. As a result, we have an epidemic of obesity in this country.

For those who do eat breakfast, it commonly consists of something such as bagels with cream cheese, doughnuts, and coffee. Try healthy alternatives for breakfast such as high-fiber cereals with soy milk, skim milk, or rice milk. You may add berries or other fruit for extra flavor and nutrition. Or try plain low-fat yogurt without any added sugar, and simply add the fruit or berries to the yogurt. Whole-grain low-sugar granola is also healthy, as well as hot cereal such as old-fashioned oatmeal or oat bran. Or you may enjoy whole-grain blueberry pancakes

Another healthy breakfast consists of toasted whole-grain bread with low-sugar fruit spread or a mixture of olive oil and butter (see recipe on page 3) on top. A very healthy breakfast that I commonly eat consists of an omelet with one free-range egg with yolk plus two to three egg whites. I cook the eggs with extra virgin olive oil and then add vegetables such as onions, peppers, mushrooms, and tomatoes. I also like Ezekiel bread, millet bread, or any other type of whole-grain bread made as French toast, sprinkled with cinnamon, and served with blueberries on top.

Instead of grabbing a doughnut on the way to work, grab a piece of fruit—I recommend you eat a piece every morning. If you are in the habit of drinking a cup of coffee in the car, try a protein shake for breakfast using soy, whey, or rice protein mixed with water or soy milk. Just add your favorite fresh berries such as blueberries, strawberries, raspberries, or blackberries, and blend in a blender. I often grind one tablespoon of flaxseeds in a coffee grinder and blend this in with the shake.

Start your day with a healthy breakfast, and reap the health benefits of the most important meal of the day. And as you go through the rest your day, ask yourself, *What Would Jesus Eat?*

When you think of the typical American diet, that is not the way Jesus ate. Instead, the way we are eating has put us into the fast lane of health decline. Our modern fast-food diets are high in salt, low in fiber, very high in fat and sugar, and virtually void of nutrients—and that is *not* the way Jesus ate.

If you truly want to follow Jesus in every area of your life, you cannot ignore your eating habits. It is an area in which you can follow Him daily and reap great rewards for doing so. Following Jesus in your diet requires a commitment to change, a commitment to be all that God created you to be, and a commitment to yield your desires to God's instruction. God, in turn, will honor your heartfelt commitment by giving you more energy, better health, and a greater sense of well being.

Are you willing to make a commitment to follow Jesus' example and eat the way He ate? If you are, then let's begin cooking.

The eating habits that were the foundation of Jesus' diet were:
choosing untampered, nutrient-dense foods;
avoiding foods that have been processed or refined;
choosing foods that are in their natural, fresh state.

Making the Change to a Mediterranean Healthstyle

These are the ten major steps I recommend for a person who wants to change from a typical American way of eating to a Mediterranean way of eating:

1. Eliminate all processed foods from your cupboards, and start over. Begin to buy whole-grain products and fresh fruits and vegetables. Stock your shelves with olive oil, nuts, seeds, and whole grains.

2. Cook and bake with whole-grain products. Eat more fresh fruits, vegetables, beans, legumes, and nuts.

3. Substitute olive oil for butter, margarine, salad dressings, and other oils.

4. Avoid all fried or deep-fried foods.

5. Limit cheese intake to Parmesan or feta cheese (used on main dishes or salads). Do not eat blocks of cheese.

6. Eat yogurt with fruit, or sweeten it with Stevia (a natural substitute for sugar with no harmful side effects).

7. Choose fish and poultry over red meat, and eat meat sparingly. Cut out sugary sweets.

8. Enjoy a glass of red wine with lunch or dinner.

9. Exercise regularly—walk more.

10. Make dining an experience that you enjoy with others. Slow down your eating, savor your food, and enjoy sharing life with family and friends.

APPETIZERS

& SAUCES

For the LORD your God is bringing you into a good land, a land of brooks of water, of fountains and springs, that flow out of valleys and hills; a land of wheat and barley, of vines and fig trees and pomegranates, a land of olive oil and honey; a land in which you will eat bread without scarcity, in which you will lack nothing; a land whose stones are iron and out of whose hills you can dig copper. When you have eaten and are full, then you shall bless the LORD your God for the good land which He has given you. (Deut. 8:7–10)

Appetizers should be served before meals with drinks or as a light snack throughout the day. They help to take the edge off hunger.

Today's Americans tend to eat alone or eat while rushed and stressed. Eating an appetizer before the meal can help you to wind down before you eat, eliminating much of the stress of your daily lifestyle. This, in turn, enables you to enjoy the meal in a pleasant, relaxing setting. It is actually good to have an appetizer before both lunch and dinner, since most of us eat on the run and chew each bite only a few times, washed down with a soft drink or tea. Eating appetizers in a relaxed atmosphere will allow you to slow down so you can feel the sense of fullness before you have eaten too much. You see, most people can eat a full meal in ten minutes, so you often have overeaten before your body has been able to signal you that you are full, since it takes about twenty minutes for this to occur.

Many of us eat because we are stressed, bored, rushed, depressed, anxious—not necessarily because we are hungry. By winding down, relaxing, slowing down, and eating with friends and family in a pleasant atmosphere, you will be less likely to overeat because of stress. Start with a simple, flavorful, diverse appetizer that is not too filling. It is intended just to take the edge off your appetite and set the stage for optimal digestion and absorption.

One of the major sources of high-quality protein from the plant world is the soybean.

Olive Oil Butter

This is a basic. It is delicious—but use it sparingly.

½ cup extra virgin olive oil
½ cup (1 stick) butter, melted or softened

Combine the extra virgin olive oil and butter in a mixing bowl, blender, or food processor. Blend until smooth. Chill, covered, until firm.

Yield: about 1 cup
See page 111 of *What Would Jesus Eat?* by Don Colbert

Edamame

**Edamame (pronounced ed-ah-MAH-may) are
highly nutritious, easily digested soybean varieties
which are eaten at the green stage as a vegetable.**

1 (10-ounce) package frozen unshelled soybeans, thawed
Celtic salt to taste

Place the soybeans in a medium microwave-safe bowl. Cover with water. Microwave on High for 2 to 3 minutes; drain. Remove soybeans from pods and sprinkle with Celtic salt.

Yield: 3 or 4 servings
Melanee Bandy

One of the things many people discover as they begin to eat whole and natural foods is that they enjoy the taste of fresh food as never before. The truth is, that many people in our nation have grown accustomed to eating foods that are laden with salt, sugar, additives, hydrogenated fats, and other items used in processing food. As a nation, we seem to have forgotten what whole fresh food tastes like.

Mediterranean Canapé Spread
Serve with crackers or spread on sandwich bread.

½ cup Olive Oil Butter, softened (page 3)

½ teaspoon oregano

½ teaspoon basil

½ teaspoon garlic powder

Combine Olive Oil Butter, oregano, basil, and garlic powder in a mixing bowl, food processor, or blender. Blend until smooth. Chill, covered, until firm. Serve with crackers.

Yield: 12 servings

Adapted from a recipe found on *RecipeSource.com*

Spicy Yogurt Sauce
This sauce makes an excellent topping for grilled chicken, fish or lamb.

8 ounces plain yogurt

1 garlic clove, minced

1 tablespoon vinegar

½ teaspoon Celtic salt

½ teaspoon cumin

1 cup coriander leaves, chopped

Combine the yogurt, garlic, vinegar, salt, cumin, and coriander in a mixing bowl or blender. Blend until smooth. Chill before serving.

Yield: 1½ cups

See page 106 of *What Would Jesus Eat?* by Don Colbert

Mediterranean Cheese Tart

The phyllo shell is as savory as the filling.

8   sheets frozen phyllo dough, thawed

¼   cup melted Olive Oil Butter (p. 3)

5   tablespoons grated fresh Parmesan cheese

½   cup chopped onion

1   teaspoon minced fresh rosemary, or ¼ teaspoon crushed
    dried rosemary

1   tablespoon extra virgin olive oil

5   ounces frozen chopped spinach, thawed, drained

⅓   cup toasted pine nuts or chopped walnuts

1   egg

1   cup ricotta cheese

½   cup crumbled feta cheese

¼   cup chopped sun-dried tomatoes

¼   teaspoon coarsely ground black pepper

Unfold the phyllo dough; cover with a damp towel to keep from drying out. Place 2 sheets of phyllo on a dry working surface. Brush with 1 table-spoon of the Olive Oil Butter; sprinkle with 1 tablespoon of the Parmesan cheese. Repeat the phyllo, Olive Oil Butter, and Parmesan cheese layers three times. Trim the stacked dough into an 11-inch circle with kitchen shears. Generously grease the bottom and side of a 9-inch springform pan. Ease the dough circle evenly into the prepared pan, pleating as necessary and being careful not to tear the dough. Cover the dough-lined pan with a damp towel until ready to fill.

Sauté the onion and rosemary in extra virgin olive oil in a medium saucepan over medium-low heat for 5 minutes or until onion is tender. Stir in the spinach and pine nuts. Spread the spinach mixture in the phyllo shell. Place the egg in a medium mixing bowl and beat lightly. Stir in the ricotta, feta, sun-dried tomatoes, and black pepper. Spread the ricotta mixture carefully over the spinach mixture. Sprinkle with the remaining 1 tablespoon Parmesan cheese.

Set the pan on a baking sheet. Bake at 350 degrees for 35 to 40 minutes or until center appears nearly set when lightly shaken. Remove to a wire rack to cool for 5 minutes. Use a kitchen knife to loosen the tart from the side of the pan. Let cool for 15 to 30 minutes longer. Remove the side of the pan. Serve warm.

Yield: 12 servings
Adapted from a recipe found on *RecipeSource.com*

Marinara Sauce
This flavorful sauce does not need to be cooked!

1   (8-ounce) can reduced-salt tomato sauce
2 or 3   fresh tomatoes, chopped
2 or 3   garlic cloves, minced
1   cup onions, chopped
3   tablespoons extra virgin olive oil
1   teaspoon oregano
2   tablespoons fresh parsley, chopped
2   teaspoons basil
Celtic salt and frest ground black pepper to taste

Combine the tomato sauce, tomatoes, garlic, onions, olive oil, oregano, parsley, basil, salt, and pepper in a bowl; mix well. Serve over hot pasta.

Yield: 3 to 4 cups
See page 216 of *What Would Jesus Eat?* by Don Colbert

Antipasto Mediterranean

½ cup wine vinegar

¼ cup extra virgin olive oil

2 tablespoons sugar (or 12 to 18 drops of Stevia)

1 tablespoon Celtic salt

½ teaspoon oregano

¼ cup water

¼ teaspoon fresh ground black pepper

2 carrots, peeled, cut in ½-inch pieces

2 ribs celery, cut in 1-inch pieces

1 small head cauliflower, broken in pieces

1 green bell pepper, sliced lengthwise

1 (4-ounce) jar button mushrooms, drained

1 (4-ounce) jar black olives, drained

1 (4-ounce) jar stuffed green olives, drained

1 (4-ounce) jar pickled onions

Combine the vinegar, extra virgin olive oil, sugar, salt, oregano, water, black pepper, and carrots in a large skillet over medium heat. Simmer, covered, for 2 minutes. Add the celery and cauliflower and simmer, covered, for 2 minutes longer. Add the bell pepper, mushrooms, black and green olives, and undrained onions; simmer, covered, for 1 minute longer. Cool. Chill, covered, for 24 hours. Drain and serve with wooden picks.

Yield: 16 to 24 servings
Adapted from a recipe found on *CookbooksOnline*.com

Cheese Spread

**If fresh herbs are not available, use one teaspoon
each of dried thyme, parsley, and dill.**

½ cup fresh curd cheese (or farmer's cheese, fat-free cream cheese,
or yogurt cheese)

4 garlic cloves, minced

2 tablespoons extra virgin olive oil

1 tablespoon chopped fresh thyme

1 tablespoon chopped fresh dill

1 tablespoon chopped fresh parsley

Celtic salt

Combine the cheese, garlic, olive oil, thyme, dill, and parsley in a bowl
and mix well. Salt to taste. Serve with nutty, whole grain breads.

Yield: 2 cups

See page 75 of *What Would Jesus Eat?* by Don Colbert

Hummus

This recipe is easily doubled.

2 cups dried chickpeas

½ cup tahini (or less depending on taste)

2 tablespoons extra virgin olive oil

1 garlic clove, minced

Juice of 2 medium lemons

½ to 1 teaspoon Celtic salt

½ teaspoon cumin

Cover chickpeas with water and soak for 8 to 10 hours. Drain well. Combine
the drained chickpeas and 1 quart fresh water in a kettle over medium-high

heat. Bring to a boil. Reduce heat and simmer for 1 to 2 hours or until chickpeas are tender. Drain well. Purée the chickpeas in a blender or food processor. Add the tahini, olive oil, garlic, lemon juice, salt, and cumin; blend until smooth. Adjust seasoning. Serve immediately, or place in an airtight container in the refrigerator until serving time (will keep about five days).

Yield: about 4 cups

See page 215 of *What Would Jesus Eat?* by Don Colbert

Celtic salt is a sea salt. It is a non processed natural salt with all its nutrients still intact, unlike common table salt that has been processed, and often mixed with aluminum to make it more soluble.

Toasted Pumpkin Seeds

Store in an airtight container to keep on hand for a savory snack.

Pumpkin seeds
Celtic salt to taste
Chili powder (optional)
Garlic powder (optional)

Scoop the seeds from a fresh medium-sized pumpkin. Remove all pulp, and place the seeds in a strainer; rinse. Arrange the seeds on a lightly oiled baking sheet in a single layer; spray lightly with olive oil cooking spray. Sprinkle with salt, chili powder, and garlic powder. Bake at 250 to 300 degrees for ½ to 1½ hours or until seeds are light brown and crispy. Check often while baking, stirring occasionally.

Adapted from a recipe found on *SeedsofKnowledge.com*

Brenda Hyde lives in Michigan with her husband and three children. She is editor of *SeedsofKnowledge.com* and *OldFashionedHolidays.com*.

Basil Purée

**It's delicious on grilled chicken or fish, stirred into soups,
or mixed with sun-dried tomatoes and broiled on bread.**

4   tablespoons extra virgin olive oil
8   cups basil leaves, washed, dried

Combine the olive oil and basil leaves in the container of a blender or
food processor and process until smooth. Remove the basil mixture to a
clean quart jar. Chill, covered, until time to use. Stir before using. After
using, top the remaining basil mixture with a thin layer of olive oil. It
will keep, covered, in the refrigerator for up to one year.

Yield: 3 to 4 cups
Adapted from a recipe found on *SeedsofKnowledge.com*

Basil and Tomato Bruschette

**The traditional recipe for bruschette calls for the
bread to be drenched in olive oil. Here we use less oil
and add a tomato mixture for moisture.**

2   large ripe tomatoes, peeled, seeded, diced
2   tablespoons fresh oregano, chopped
24 to 36 basil leaves, torn into small pieces
12 (1-inch) slices crusty Italian bread
12 garlic cloves, peeled, halved lengthwise
⅓ to ½ cup extra virgin olive oil
Celtic salt and freshly ground black pepper to taste
Grated Parmesan cheese to taste

Combine the tomatoes, oregano, and basil in a bowl; mix well. Toast the bread slices over a grill, under a broiler, or in a preheated 425-degree oven for a few minutes or until beginning to brown around the edges. Remove from heat and rub while still warm with the cut sides of the garlic. Brush with olive oil and top with the tomato mixture. Sprinkle with salt, pepper, and Parmesan cheese. Heat under the broiler for 1 minute or until top is hot and light brown.

Yield: 6 to 12 servings
Adapted from a recipe found on SeedsofKnowledge.com

Basil Walnut Paste

**This recipe yields enough paste for about
two pounds of poultry or fish.**

1   cup lightly packed fresh basil leaves
3   garlic cloves, peeled
¾   cup walnut pieces
¼   cup grated Parmesan cheese
2   teaspoons red wine or herb vinegar
1   tablespoon extra virgin olive oil

Place the basil in a food processor container. Add the garlic, processing constantly for about 15 seconds or until basil and garlic are finely chopped. Add the walnuts, Parmesan cheese, vinegar, and olive oil. Process for about 20 seconds to make a rough paste. Rub evenly over poultry, fish, or vegetables just before grilling.

Yield: about 1 cup
Adapted from a recipe found on SeedsofKnowledge.com

Basil Butter

**For a nice simple appetizer, serve at room temperature
with grilled pieces of French bread.**

¼ cup (½ stick) butter, softened

¼ cup extra virgin olive oil

1 or 2 garlic cloves, minced

1 teaspoon fresh lemon juice

1 tablespoon fresh basil, finely chopped

¼ teaspoon Celtic salt

Pepper to taste

Cream the butter and olive oil in a mixing bowl until light and smooth. Beat in the garlic and lemon juice. Mash in the basil. Season with salt and pepper. Chill, covered, until firm. Bring to room temperature before serving.

Yield: ½ cup

Adapted from a recipe found on SeedsofKnowledge.com

Light Herbed Cheese Dip

**The fresh herbs make this dip especially flavorful—but you
may use smaller amounts of dried herbs if you don't have fresh ones.**

8 ounces low-fat cream cheese, softened

¼ cup plain yogurt

2 tablespoons fresh dill, chopped

2 tablespoons fresh parsley, chopped

2 small green onions, chopped

½ teaspoon minced garlic

½ teaspoon Celtic salt

Combine the cream cheese and yogurt in a food processor or blender container and process for 1 to 2 minutes. Add the dill, parsley, green onions, garlic, and salt; process for 30 seconds or just until blended. Serve with raw vegetables.

Yield: 1½ cups

Adapted from a recipe found on SeedsofKnowledge.com

Yogurt Cheese

Use Yogurt Cheese as a spread for fresh vegetables, crackers, or bread. If you would like to use fresh herbs, substitute ½ teaspoon each of snipped fresh basil, oregano, thyme, and marjoram for the dried herbs.

8   ounces plain low-fat yogurt

⅛   teaspoon each thyme or marjoram, basil, oregano, and Italian seasoning

1   tablespoon grated Parmesan cheese

Combine the yogurt and herbs in a small bowl; blend until smooth. Stir in the Parmesan cheese. Set a small strainer over a bowl and line the strainer with clean cheesecloth. Spoon the yogurt mixture into the cheesecloth-lined strainer. Let drain in the refrigerator, covered, for 8 to 10 hours.

Turn the yogurt mixture carefully onto a serving plate and remove the cheesecloth. Discard the liquid. It may be stored, covered, in the refrigerator for up to 1 week.

Yield: ½ cup

Marinated Mushrooms and Zucchini

Marinating vegetables in a sealed plastic bag
makes it easy to turn the mixture.

8   ounces small whole fresh mushrooms
2   small zucchini, sliced
1   small red bell pepper, chopped
¼   cup fresh lemon juice
2   tablespoons extra virgin olive oil
1   tablespoon sugar (or 6 to 9 drops of Stevia)
¼   teaspoon Celtic salt
¼   teaspoon tarragon or oregano
¼   teaspoon freshly ground black pepper
1   garlic clove, minced

Combine the mushrooms, zucchini, and bell pepper in a resealable plastic bag and place the bag in a deep bowl. Combine the lemon juice, olive oil, sugar, salt, tarragon, black pepper, and garlic in a small bowl; mix well. Pour the lemon juice mixture over vegetables in the bag; seal. Marinate in the refrigerator for 8 to 10 hours, turning bag occasionally. Arrange in a serving dish and serve with wooden picks.

Yield: about 10 servings

Our goal when it comes to fat consumption should be twofold: first, to decrease the percentage of our diet from fat, and second, to make sure that nearly all of our fat-related calories come from natural foods and monounsaturated oils, such as olive oil.

Apple-Stuffed Mushrooms

Walnuts, feta cheese, and apples are a classic combination.

32 medium to large fresh mushrooms, washed

4   tablespoons finely chopped celery

½   cup minced peeled apple

2   tablespoons dry bread crumbs

1½ tablespoons chopped fresh parsley

2   tablespoons chopped toasted walnuts

1   tablespoon crumbled feta cheese

2   teaspoons fresh lemon juice

Remove the mushroom stems. Finely chop enough of the stems to make ⅓ cup of chopped stems. Coat a skillet with olive oil cooking spray and place over medium-high heat until hot. Combine the celery and the chopped mushroom stems in the hot skillet; sauté for about 3 minutes or until tender. Remove from heat. Combine the celery mixture, apple, bread crumbs, parsley, walnuts, feta cheese, and lemon juice in a bowl; mix well. Fill each mushroom cap with a small amount of the apple mixture. Arrange the filled mushrooms on a baking sheet. Bake at 350 degrees for 15 to 20 minutes or until browned and bubbly.

Yield: 32 pieces

Black Bean Hummus

16 ounces dry black beans, cooked, drained
4   tablespoons extra virgin olive oil
Juice of 1 lemon
2   garlic cloves, minced
Celtic salt
1   teaspoon cumin
Freshly ground black pepper to taste
Tahini to taste

Combine the black beans, olive oil, lemon juice, garlic, salt, cumin, pepper, and tahini in a food processor container; process until smooth. Serve at room temperature.

Yield: 2 cups

Baked Sweet Onions

4   large sweet Vidalia onions, peeled
Celtic salt and freshly ground black pepper to taste
4   teaspoons extra virgin olive oil

Arrange the onions in a baking dish. Add 1 inch of water. Bake, uncovered, at 250 degrees for 2 hours or until onions are tender.

Remove from oven; peel off the brown skins and cut off the roots. Arrange the onions on a serving platter and season each one with salt, pepper, and 1 teaspoon extra virgin olive oil.

Yield: 4 servings
Adapted from a recipe found on *WhatsCooking.com*

Avocado Olive Dip

3 ripe avocados, peeled, seeded, mashed

1 (6-ounce) can black olives, drained, sliced

1 (4-ounce) can chile or jalapeño peppers, drained

7 or 8 small green onions, chopped

3 large tomatoes, chopped

3 or 4 garlic cloves, minced

6 tablespoons extra virgin olive oil

2 tablespoons fresh lemon juice

5 or 6 fresh basil leaves, finely chopped

Combine the avocados, olives, chile peppers, green onions, tomatoes, garlic, olive oil, lemon juice, and basil in a large bowl; mix well. Chill, covered, for at least 2 hours.

Yield: about 3 cups

Adapted from a recipe found on *WhatsCooking.com*

Canned beans tend to be high in salt. If you absolutely must use canned beans, first rinse them in clean water to remove some of the salt.

Baked Portobello Mushrooms

4   large portobello mushrooms, cleaned, stemmed

¼   cup extra virgin olive oil

2   garlic cloves, minced

2   tablespoons balsamic vinegar

½   cup fresh thyme leaves, chopped

Celtic salt and ground pepper to taste

Make several shallow cuts in the center of each mushroom where the stem was attached. Heat the olive oil and garlic in a small saucepan over medium heat for about 8 to 10 minutes, stirring frequently. Remove from heat. Strain the olive oil and let cool; discard the garlic.

Combine the garlic-flavored olive oil, balsamic vinegar, thyme, salt, and pepper in a small bowl; mix well. Arrange the mushrooms, cut side down, on a baking pan that has been lightly sprayed with nonstick cooking spray. Drizzle the olive oil mixture over the mushrooms. Bake at 350 degrees for 15 minutes; turn mushrooms over and bake for 10 to 15 minutes longer or until tender.

Yield: 4 servings

Adapted from a recipe found on *WhatsCooking.com*

Extra virgin olive oil is oil from the first pressing of olives; the oil is extracted, filtered and undergoes no further refining. It is the highest quality oil. Very strict guidelines exist for a product to be named "extra virgin."

Red Pepper Dip

Serve this savory dip with fresh vegetables or over toasted bread.

½   cup red bell peppers, roasted
1   teaspoon basil
1   garlic clove, minced
1   cup fat-free cottage cheese

Combine the roasted peppers, basil, and garlic in a blender or food processor. Process until chopped. Add the cottage cheese; process until well blended. Chill, covered, for at least 1 hour.

Yield: about 1 cup

Mustard Pecans

**Store these pecans in airtight containers and
they should keep for about a week.**

⅓   cup Dijon mustard
3   tablespoons honey
¼   cup extra virgin olive oil
½   teaspoon Celtic salt
¼   teaspoon freshly ground black pepper
1   pound pecan halves

Line the bottom of a large baking pan with aluminum foil. Combine the mustard, honey, olive oil, salt, and pepper in a shallow bowl; whisk well. Add the pecans; stir until coated. Spread a single layer of pecans on the foil-lined baking sheet. Bake at 300 degrees for 10 minutes. Stir to turn and bake for 10 minutes longer. Watch closely, as pecans burn easily. Cool completely.

Yield: 1 pound

Spinach Balls

2 (10-ounce) packages frozen spinach, cooked
2 cups herb-flavored stuffing mix
1 large onion, finely chopped
6 eggs, well beaten
¾ cup extra virgin olive oil
½ cup grated fresh Parmesan cheese
Cayenne pepper to taste
1 garlic clove, minced
1 teaspoon Celtic salt

Drain the spinach, taking care to squeeze out all moisture. Combine the spinach, stuffing mix, onion, eggs, olive oil, Parmesan cheese, cayenne pepper, garlic, and salt in a large bowl; mix well. Shape the mixture into ¾-inch balls and arrange on a baking sheet that has been sprayed with olive oil cooking spray. Bake at 325 degrees for 15 to 20 minutes or until lightly browned.

Yield: 6 to 8 servings

Cilantro Salsa

Served as a dip with pita bread or over grilled fish.

1   large bunch cilantro, chopped
2   garlic cloves, minced
¼   cup water
½   cup extra virgin olive oil
3   teaspoons fresh lime juice
¼   teaspoon cayenne pepper
¼   teaspoon coriander
Celtic salt to taste

Combine the cilantro and garlic in a blender or food processor container. Purée with the water and olive oil. Add the lime juice, cayenne pepper, coriander, and salt; process briefly until well mixed.

Yield: about 1 cup

For maximum health benefits, olive oil that is consumed should be extra virgin or virgin olive oil. If a bottle of olive oil is not labeled as "extra virgin" or "virgin," then the oil has been refined in some way.

Just one tablespoon of olive oil has the following:

Calories	*119*
Vitamin E	*3-30 milligrams*
Monounsaturated fatty acids (oleic)	*56-83 %*
Polyunsaturated unfatty acids (linoleic)	*3.5-20%*
Saturated fatty acids	*8.0-23.5 %*

Marinated Asparagus with Fennel Dressing

**Vinegar, mustard, and lime juice add an
appealing sharpness to this vegetable dish.**

½ cup extra virgin olive oil

½ cup red wine vinegar

2 teaspoons dry mustard

¾ teaspoon dried fennel

1 teaspoon fresh lime juice

2 tablespoons finely chopped fresh parsley

1 pound fresh asparagus, washed, cut into 2-inch pieces

Combine the olive oil, vinegar, mustard, fennel, lime juice, and parsley in a large glass dish; whisk to blend. Add the asparagus and marinate, covered, in the refrigerator for about 4 hours before serving.

Yield: 2 to 3 cups

Sun-Dried Tomato Dip

10 oil-packed sun-dried tomatoes, drained, chopped

8 ounces low-fat cream cheese, softened

1 cup low-fat sour cream

1 teaspoon Celtic salt

½ teaspoon freshly ground black pepper

2 scallions, sliced

Combine the sun-dried tomatoes, cream cheese, sour cream, salt, pepper, and scallions in a food processor container. Process until desired consistency.

Yield: 2 cups

Marinated Broccoli

2   pounds fresh broccoli
¾   cup balsamic vinegar
½   cup extra virgin olive oil
3   tablespoons water
2   garlic cloves, minced
1   teaspoon dill
2   teaspoons Celtic salt
½   teaspoon freshly ground black pepper

Wash broccoli and cut into florets; place in a large bowl. Combine the vinegar, olive oil, water, garlic, dill, salt, and pepper in a small bowl; whisk well. Pour over the broccoli. Chill, covered, for at least 8 hours, stirring occasionally.

Yield: 8 to 12 servings

Herbed Potato Skins

3   medium baking potatoes, scrubbed
Extra virgin olive oil
4   ounces feta cheese, crumbled
1½ teaspoons oregano
½   teaspoon basil
¼   teaspoon rosemary
½   teaspoon garlic salt

Preheat the oven to 400 degrees. Pierce potatoes with a fork or sharp knife and rub with oil. Bake for 1 hour or until done; cool slightly. Cut potatoes in half lengthwise. Scoop out the pulp, leaving a ¼-inch shell (save pulp for another use). Cut skins in half lengthwise, then cut in half crosswise. Arrange skins on a baking sheet and brush with olive oil. Bake for 5 minutes. Combine the feta cheese, oregano, basil, rosemary, and garlic salt in a small bowl; mix well. Remove potato skins from oven and top with the feta cheese mixture. Drizzle with additional olive oil. Turn on broiler and broil for 2 to 3 minutes or until cheese is bubbly.

Yield: 24 skins
Adapted from a recipe found on *SeedsofKnowledge.com*

Black-Eyed Pea Dip

Serve with tortilla chips, bagel chips, or toasted pita bread.

16 ounces black-eyed peas, cooked, drained
3   green onions, chopped with tops
½   cup sour cream
1   teaspoon garlic salt
½   cup salsa

Place all but ⅓ cup of the black-eyed peas in a blender or food processor container; process until smooth. Blend in the onions, sour cream, and garlic salt. Remove to a bowl; stir in the reserved peas and the salsa.

Yield: 8 to 12 servings
Adapted from a recipe found on *SeedsofKnowledge.com*

Zucchini Appetizers

Refrigerate any leftover appetizers.

3 cups thinly sliced unpeeled zucchini

1 cup biscuit baking mix

½ cup grated fresh Parmesan cheese

½ cup finely chopped onion

4 slightly beaten eggs

½ teaspoon Celtic salt

2 tablespoons snipped parsley

½ teaspoon dried marjoram or oregano leaves

Dash of pepper

1 finely chopped garlic clove

1 cup extra virgin olive oil

Preheat the oven to 350 degrees. Combine the zucchini, baking mix, Parmesan cheese, onion, eggs, salt, parsley, marjoram, pepper, garlic, and olive oil in a large bowl; mix well. Spread the zucchini mixture in a greased 9x13x2-inch baking dish. Bake for about 25 minutes or until golden brown. Remove from oven; cool slightly. Cut into 1x2-inch rectangles and serve.

Yield: 4 dozen

Adapted from a recipe found on *CookbooksOnline.com*

SOUPS

& SALADS

We remember the fish which we ate freely in Egypt, the cucumbers, the melons, the leeks, the onions, and the garlic. (Num. 11:5)

Soups were a vital part of the foods that were eaten during the days of Jesus. In fact, we read in the Bible that Esau forfeited his entire birthright to his brother, Jacob, for a bowl of soup.

During biblical times, especially when food was scarce, soup would usually constitute the entire meal and contained beans, legumes, lentils, vegetables, garlic, and onions. People often ate bread with their soup. Grains and beans are incomplete proteins by themselves. However, when grains and beans are combined, they then become a complete protein, supplying all of the essential amino acids. So soup and bread together made a remarkably healthy meal in Jesus' day, as they do now.

If you use meat in your soups, it should be very lean and preferably free-range. The protein sources consumed primarily during the days of Jesus were fish, chicken, and lamb.

Salads are commonly consumed in Israel as well as other Mediterranean countries. The salad leaves, however, vary from country to country, with a wide range of flavor, color, and taste. The standard salad in America primarily contains iceberg lettuce, which has a very low nutrient value and is essentially void of fiber, buttery croutons, excessive amounts of cheese, and pasty salad dressing composed primarily of processed polyunsaturated fats, which are full of lipid peroxides. In Mediterranean countries most salads contain rich, dark-green salad leaves and bright, contrasting, colorful vegetables, creating a vibrant, colorful salad.

For the most nutritious salads, choose a variety of salad leaves, like romaine lettuce, chicory, oak leaf lettuce, red leaf lettuce, dandelion leaves, and spinach, as well as other wonderful vibrant green leafy vegetables. Add some vine-ripened tomatoes, peppers, onions, carrots, beans, and vegetables. You may try a small amount of Parmesan cheese grated over the salad.

Salad dressing in Jesus' day was made of extra virgin olive oil mixed with flavorful vinegars like balsamic vinegar, apple cider vinegar, and red wine vinegar. Refer to page 38 for vinegar and olive oil salad dressing recipe. This was combined with lemon juice, garlic, salt, and other herbs to create a robust, tangy flavor. These salads were a colorful display of vegetables full of phytonutrients, antioxidants, vitamins, minerals and living enzymes as well as the health-promoting fat, extra virgin olive oil, which helps prevent heart disease.

Dinner is a good time to have a large salad of dark green lettuce (such as romaine) and add other fresh vegetables as desired, such as carrots, onions, tomatoes, and cucumbers. The more brilliantly colored, the better!

Mediterranean Lentil Soup

5   cups lentils, sorted, washed
3   quarts water
1½ large onions, chopped
2   tablespoons extra virgin olive oil
1   green bell pepper, chopped
1   teaspoon Celtic salt
¼   teaspoon freshly ground black pepper
1   teaspoon cumin
1   cup fresh cilantro, chopped
5   garlic cloves, minced
½   cup fresh lime juice

Combine the lentils and water in a kettle over high heat and bring to a boil. Reduce heat and simmer while preparing other ingredients. Sauté the onions in half of the olive oil in a saucepan over medium heat for about 8 minutes. Add the bell pepper and sauté for a minute or two longer. Add the onion mixture to the lentils. Simmer for 30 minutes. Season with salt, pepper, and cumin. Simmer for 20 minutes longer. Stir in the cilantro; remove kettle from heat.

Combine the garlic, lime juice, and the remaining 1 tablespoon olive oil in a food processor or blender and blend well. Add garlic mixture and lime juice to the lentil mixture. Mix well and serve.

Yield: 6 servings

Tomato Salad

4   tomatoes, thinly sliced

1   cucumber, peeled, thinly sliced

¼   cup sliced black olives

¼   cup sweet onion, finely chopped

1   cup celery, sliced

¼   cup chopped mint

3   tablespoons chopped parsley

2   garlic cloves, minced

2   tablespoons extra virgin olive oil

2   tablespoons balsamic vinegar

Celtic salt and freshly ground pepper to taste

Place tomatoes and cucumbers in a large bowl. Add the olives, onions, celery, mint, and parsley; toss to combine. Combine the garlic, olive oil, vinegar, salt, and pepper in a small bowl and whisk well. Add the vinegar mixture to the tomato mixture and toss lightly.

Yield: 6 servings

The two foremost grains used in the Old Testament were barley and wheat. Wheat is actually mentioned fifty-one times in the Scriptures.

Barley Soup

1   cup barley
½   cup lentils
6   cups water
2   onions, chopped
2   tablespoons extra virgin olive oil
1   tablespoon dried parsley
1   teaspoon cumin
Celtic salt and freshly ground pepper to taste

Combine the barley, lentils, water, onions, olive oil, parsley, cumin, salt, and pepper in a large saucepan over high heat; bring to a boil. Reduce heat and simmer, partially covered, for 1 hour, stirring occasionally.

Yield: 6 to 8 servings

Lebanese Fresh Fruit Salad

**To prevent apple and bananas from turning brown,
serve immediately after tossing.**

1   honeydew melon
½   pineapple
1   orange
1   apple or pear
2   bananas

Slice the honeydew, pineapple, orange, apple, and bananas into bite-size pieces in a large bowl. Toss lightly.

Yield: 6 servings
Adapted from a recipe found on *RecipeSource.com*

Mediterranean Orange Salad

2   cups torn spinach

1   (11-ounce) can mandarin oranges, drained

1   cup red onion rings

6   ounces feta cheese, cubed

½   cup pitted ripe olives

2   tablespoons extra virgin olive oil

2   tablespoons fresh lemon juice

Celtic salt and pepper to taste

Place the spinach, oranges, onion rings, feta cheese, and olives in a large bowl and toss to combine. Combine the olive oil, lemon juice, salt, and pepper in a small bowl and whisk well. Add the olive oil mixture to the spinach mixture. Toss and serve.

Yield: 4 servings

Adapted from a recipe found on *CookbooksOnline.com*

Tuna Salad

2 to 3 ounces water-packed tuna, drained

Chopped onions

Chopped celery

1   cup Chopped tomatoes

1   cup Sliced cucumbers

Romaine

Vinegar and Olive Oil Salad Dressing (see page 38)

Place the tuna, onions, celery, tomatoes, and cucumbers in a bowl; toss to combine. Serve on a bed of romaine, with Vinegar and Olive Oil Salad Dressing.

See page 213 of *What Would Jesus Eat?* by Don Colbert

Mediterranean Bean Salad

1   cup navy beans
1   (6-ounce) can tuna, drained, broken into chunks
1   small onion, finely chopped
½   medium cucumber, peeled, thinly sliced
2   garlic cloves, crushed
2   tablespoons dried parsley
½   teaspoon tarragon
2   teaspoons Celtic salt
½   teaspoon freshly ground pepper
½   cup extra virgin olive oil
1   tablespoon fresh lemon juice

Place the beans and enough water to cover in a saucepan over high heat. Bring to a rapid boil. Cover, remove from heat, and let stand for 1 hour; drain. Add enough fresh water to cover the beans in the saucepan over high heat. Bring to a boil. Reduce heat, cover, and simmer for 1½ hours or until beans are tender. Drain. Place the beans in a glass or ceramic salad bowl and let cool.

When beans are cooled, add the tuna, onion, cucumber, garlic, parsley, tarragon, salt, pepper, olive oil, and lemon juice. Toss gently, being careful not to mash the beans. Refrigerate until well chilled.

Yield: 4 servings
Adapted from a recipe found on *CookbooksOnline*.com

Mediterranean Rice Salad

1 tablespoon extra virgin olive oil

4 medium zucchini, cut in ¼-inch slices

1 to 2 tablespoons water

1 teaspoon basil

1 teaspoon oregano

4 cups chopped lettuce

2 cups chopped spinach

1 cup alfalfa sprouts

1 cup sliced pimento-stuffed green olives

1 cup long grain brown rice, cooked

Vinegar and Olive Oil Salad Dressing to taste (see page 38)

Heat the olive oil in a small skillet; add the zucchini to the hot oil and toss for several minutes. Remove from heat and stir in the basil and oregano. Place the lettuce, spinach, sprouts, olives, rice, and zucchini mixture in a large salad bowl; toss to combine. Add Vinegar and Olive Oil Salad Dressing and toss well.

Yield: 8 to 10 servings
Adapted from a recipe found on *CookbooksOnline.com*

Mediterranean Chicken Salad with Broccoli

Use homemade mayonnaise if possible.

4   tablespoons extra virgin olive oil
8   boneless skinless free-range chicken breasts
½   cup dry white wine
2   garlic cloves, minced
1   bunch broccoli, peeled, trimmed
1   cup mayonnaise
1   tablespoon fresh lemon juice
½   teaspoon thyme
¼   teaspoon basil
¼   teaspoon oregano
½   teaspoon Celtic salt
½   teaspoon pepper
1   medium red onion, quartered, sliced
Sliced tomatoes
Toasted slivered almonds

Heat the olive oil in a large skillet over low heat. Arrange the chicken breasts in a single layer in the skillet and add the wine. Cover tightly and cook for 15 minutes or until chicken is cooked through. Remove the chicken and cool. Add the garlic to the remaining cooking liquid in the skillet and cook over medium-low heat for 1 minute. Strain the cooking liquid; reserve both garlic and ⅓ cup of the cooking liquid. Set aside to cool.

Separate the broccoli tops into 1-inch florets; cut the remainder of the broccoli into ½-inch dice. Blanch the broccoli in boiling water for about 30 seconds; drain. Rinse under cold water; drain well.

Combine the mayonnaise, lemon juice, thyme, basil, and oregano in a small bowl; whisk well. Whisk in the reserved garlic and cooking liquid and season with salt and pepper. Chop the chicken into ¾-inch cubes. Combine the chicken, broccoli, and onion in a large salad bowl. Add the mayonnaise mixture and toss well. Chill, covered, for 2 to 10 hours. At serving time, arrange the tomato slices around the edge of the salad and sprinkle with toasted almonds.

Yield: 8 to 10 servings

Adapted from a recipe found on *CookbooksOnline.com*

Yogurt Salad

If you have no fresh mint, use two teaspoons dried mint.

2   cups low-fat plain yogurt
2   tablespoons minced fresh mint
2   cloves garlic, crushed
2   large cucumbers, peeled, sliced
Watercress and radish slices

Combine the yogurt, mint, garlic, and cucumbers in a bowl; mix well. Serve on a bed of watercress and radish slices.

Yield: 4 to 6 servings

See page 27 of *What Would Jesus Eat?* by Don Colbert

Yogurt is highly regarded around the world as a "super food." It seems to be the mainstay in the diets of people who are traditionally long-lived such as those living in parts of Turkey, Armenia, and remote regions of the Caucasus Mountains.

Vinegar and Olive Oil Salad Dressing

6 tablespoons extra virgin olive oil

4 tablespoons balsamic vinegar

2 tablespoons fresh lemon juice

½ teaspoon Celtic salt (more if needed)

1 or 2 garlic cloves, crushed

Combine the olive oil, vinegar, lemon juice, salt, and garlic in a food processor or blender; process until well blended. Store in a sealed container in the refrigerator.

Yield: ¾ cup
See page 214 of *What Would Jesus Eat?* by Don Colbert

Chicken and Brown Rice Soup

Adjust ingredient amounts to your taste.

1 teaspoon extra virgin olive oil

Chopped onion, celery, and parsley

½ cup chopped cooked free-range chicken

½ cup cooked brown rice

½ (14-ounce) can low-sodium chicken broth

Celtic salt and pepper to taste

Heat the olive oil in a saucepan over medium-low heat. Sauté the onion, celery, and parsley in the hot oil for 5 to 10 minutes or until tender. Stir in the chicken, rice, chicken broth, salt, and pepper. Heat and serve.

Yield: 1 serving
See page 219 of *What Would Jesus Eat?* by Don Colbert

Fruit Soup

Make sure this delightful soup is very cold before serving.

1   cantaloupe, halved, seeded

1   quart strawberries

½   pound red seedless grapes

4   apples, peeled, cored, quartered

¾   cup fresh lemon juice

½   cup sugar (or 1/2 teaspoon of liquid Stevia)

6   cups water

1½ cups fresh orange juice

Scoop out the pulp of the cantaloupe with a spoon and slice it into bite-size pieces. Wash the strawberries and grapes and discard the stems. Blend the cantaloupe, strawberries, grapes, apples, ½ cup of the lemon juice, sugar, and water in a large saucepan over medium-high heat. Bring to a boil. Reduce heat and simmer, uncovered, for 15 minutes. Place the cantaloupe mixture in a food processor and purée for 30 seconds. Mix in the remaining ¼ cup lemon juice and the orange juice. Cover and chill.

Yield: 8 servings
Adapted from a recipe found on *RecipeLand.com*

Choose low-sodium, low-fat natural soup broths (available at health food stores) that are low in food additives.

Green Herb Soup

1   quart low-sodium vegetable broth
1   cup spinach, washed, shredded
1   tablespoon tomato paste
1   teaspoon Celtic salt
Freshly ground black pepper
2   tablespoons extra virgin olive oil
1   garlic clove, minced
2   teaspoons ground coriander

Pour the vegetable broth into a heavy saucepan over high heat. Bring to a boil. Stir in the spinach, tomato paste, salt, and a few grindings of black pepper. Reduce heat and simmer, covered, for about 20 minutes or until soup is thick and smooth. Heat the olive oil in a small skillet, add the garlic and coriander, and sauté until the garlic is lightly browned. Add the garlic mixture to the soup and simmer, uncovered, for 2 to 3 minutes. Serve hot.

Yield: 6 servings
Adapted from a recipe found on *RecipeLand.com*

Look for the term unpearled *on a box of barley grain or flour. This means that the barley is unprocessed and high in fiber. In contrast, the barley that is labeled "Scotch" or "pearled" has been processed and is not nearly as beneficial.*

Garlic Lentil Soup

2   quarts low-sodium vegetable broth

2   cups uncooked red lentils

1   tomato, chopped

2   teaspoons garlic, minced

2   onions, chopped

1   tablespoon extra virgin olive oil

2   teaspoons cumin

1   teaspoon Celtic salt

Freshly ground black pepper to taste

Pour the vegetable broth into a large heavy kettle over high heat. Bring to a boil. Add the lentils, tomato, garlic, and half the onions. Reduce heat to low and simmer, partially covered, for 45 minutes or until lentils are tender. Heat the olive oil in a small skillet over medium heat. Add the remaining chopped onions and cook until soft and deeply browned, stirring frequently. Remove from heat. Place the lentil mixture in a food processor and purée for one minute. Return the soup to the kettle over low heat, and stir in the cumin, salt, and black pepper. Heat for about 5 minutes. Stir in the browned onions. Serve hot.

Yield: 8 servings

Adapted from a recipe found on *RecipeLand.com*

Apple Barley Soup

2   onions, thinly sliced
2   tablespoons extra virgin olive oil
3½ cups low-sodium vegetable broth
1½ cups apple cider
⅓   cup uncooked unpearled barley
2   diced carrots
1   teaspoon thyme
¼   teaspoon marjoram
1   bay leaf
2   cups chopped, peeled apples
¼   cup minced fresh parsley
1   tablespoon fresh lemon juice
¼   teaspoon Celtic salt

Sauté the onions in olive oil in a heavy skillet or kettle over medium heat for 5 minutes. Reduce heat and cook for 10 minutes or until onions are browned. Stir in the vegetable broth, apple cider, barley, carrots, thyme, marjoram, and bay leaf. Simmer, covered, for 50 minutes or until barley is tender. Stir in the apples, parsley, lemon juice, and salt. Heat for 5 minutes or until apples are soft. Discard bay leaf and serve warm.

Yield: 6 servings
Adapted from a recipe found on *RecipeLand.com*

Greek Egg and Lemon Soup

4   cups low-sodium chicken broth

¼   cup uncooked rice

1   egg yolk

Juice of ½ lemon

Bring the chicken broth to a boil in a small saucepan over medium-high heat. Stir in the rice. Reduce heat and simmer, covered, for about 25 minutes or until rice is tender. Combine the egg yolk and lemon juice in a small bowl and beat well. Drizzle the egg mixture slowly into the simmering rice mixture, stirring constantly to separate egg into ribbons. Serve immediately.

Yield: 3 or 4 servings
Adapted from a recipe found on *RecipeLand.com*

Quick Vegetable Soup

1   quart low-sodium beef broth

1   cup tomato sauce

½   cup minced onion

1   cup chopped cabbage

2   cups chopped mixed vegetables of your choice

½   teaspoon basil, thyme, or oregano, or a mixture

⅛   teaspoon pepper

¼   cup uncooked small pasta shells or noodles

Combine the beef broth, tomato sauce, onion, cabbage, mixed vegetables, herbs, and pepper in a large kettle over medium-high heat. Bring to a boil. Add the pasta, reduce heat, and simmer for 10 minutes or until pasta is tender.

Yield: 6 servings
Adapted from a recipe found on *SeedsofKnowledge.com*

Baked Fish Chowder

3   potatoes, peeled, chopped
2   onions, chopped
Celtic salt
Freshly ground black pepper
½   cup extra virgin olive oil
Fish fillets
Skim milk
Paprika

Spray the inside of a large baking dish with olive oil cooking spray. Layer half the potatoes and onions in the bottom of the dish. Season with salt and pepper. Drizzle ¼ cup of the olive oil over the onion layer. Cover with a thick layer of fish fillets. Layer the remaining potatoes and onions over the fish layer. Season with salt and pepper and drizzle with the remaining ¼ cup olive oil. Pour in enough milk until milk level reaches top layer of onions. Sprinkle with paprika. Bake, covered with aluminum foil, at 350 degrees for 1 hour.

Yield: 6 servings

Eating a freshly baked loaf of whole-grain bread a day was, in Bible times, and is today, a healthy way to live. The bread of Jesus' time was not a traditional baker's loaf that we see in our stores today. Bread was baked on a large, flat rock, the dough stretched and twirled to make a large, flat circle. The resulting loaf was from twelve to eighteen inches across and about a half-inch thick. The pita bread we see today is a modern, thinner version of those loaves.

Garlic Soup with Cilantro Dumplings

This recipe makes about twenty-four small dumplings.

8 cups water

3 celery ribs, chopped

3 carrots, chopped

2 garlic cloves, minced

1 tablespoon fresh parsley, chopped

1 teaspoon basil

1 bay leaf

Celtic salt and freshly ground pepper to taste

1⅓ cups flour

½ teaspoon Celtic salt

¼ teaspoon freshly ground pepper

1 egg, beaten

1½ tablespoons extra virgin olive oil

⅓ cup skim milk

2 tablespoons fresh cilantro, chopped

Combine the water, celery, carrots, garlic, parsley, basil, bay leaf, and the Celtic salt and pepper to taste in a large kettle over medium-high heat. Reduce heat and simmer, covered, for about thirty minutes. To make the dumplings, combine the flour, the ½ teaspoon Celtic salt, and the ¼ teaspoon pepper in a bowl and mix well. Combine the egg, olive oil, milk, and cilantro in another bowl and mix well. Add the egg mixture to the flour mixture and stir until mixture forms a stiff batter. Shape dumpling batter into 1-inch balls and drop gently in the simmering soup. Simmer, uncovered, for about 3 minutes or until dumplings float. Serve.

Yield: 4 servings
Adapted from a recipe found on *SeedsofKnowledge.com*

Zesty Pasta Salad

Can be served with broccoli and other fresh vegetables.

16 ounces shell pasta, cooked, drained

½ to 1 cup shredded part-skim mozzarella cheese

2½ tablespoons extra virgin olive oil

2½ tablespoons balsamic vinegar

1 tablespoon chopped fresh parsley

¼ teaspoon thyme

1 teaspoon basil, or fresh basil to taste

¼ teaspoon garlic powder

½ teaspoon Celtic salt

⅛ teaspoon black pepper

Combine the pasta, mozzarella cheese, olive oil, vinegar, parsley, thyme, basil, garlic powder, salt, and pepper in large bowl and mix gently. Serve chilled or at room temperature.

Yield: 4 to 6 servings

Adapted from a recipe found on *SeedsofKnowledge.com*

Many people avoid eggs because they fear cholesterol problems. Actually, egg yolks are one of the best-known sources for choline, which is the raw material used in the body's brain function and memory. In addition to choline, eggs contain folic acid, B vitamins, antioxidants, and unsaturated fats.

Roasted Eggplant Salad

Serve with pita bread for dipping into the salad.

1   medium eggplant, halved lengthwise
4   garlic cloves, minced
¼   cup fresh lemon juice
¼   cup tahini (sesame seed paste)
Celtic salt and freshly ground black pepper to taste
Cayenne pepper to taste
Extra virgin olive oil and chopped fresh parsley to taste
Whole-grain pita bread, toasted

Place the eggplant halves cut side down on a baking sheet that has been sprayed with olive oil cooking spray. Bake at 350 degrees for about 30 minutes or until very tender. Remove from oven and let cool until eggplant is comfortable to handle. Scoop the pulp into a bowl or the container of a food processor or blender; discard the skin. Add the garlic, lemon juice, and tahini. Mash or purée until almost smooth. Season with salt, black pepper, and cayenne pepper. Remove to a serving dish. Chill, tightly covered, until serving time. Drizzle with olive oil and sprinkle with parsley before serving.

Yield: 4 to 8 servings
Adapted from a recipe found on *SeedsofKnowledge.com*

Creamy Pumpkin Soup

**The pumpkin itself is the serving bowl for this festive soup,
so be careful not to make any holes in the skin.**

1   (4½-pound) sugar pumpkin
2   cups low-sodium chicken broth
1   cup heavy cream
Celtic salt and freshly ground black pepper to taste
Dash of nutmeg
Toasted croutons

Slice the top off the pumpkin and set aside. Remove the seeds and strings from the pumpkin. Carve and scoop out the flesh of the pumpkin until the shell is about ½ inch thick. Steam the pumpkin flesh in a saucepan with an inch of water over medium heat for 20 minutes. Remove from heat, drain, and set aside to cool slightly. Heat the chicken broth in a saucepan over medium heat until warm. Purée the pumpkin flesh in a blender or food processor, and gradually stir the puréed pumpkin into the chicken broth. Slowly bring the mixture to a boil. Mix in the cream; season with salt, pepper, and nutmeg. Remove from heat. Pour the soup into the pumpkin shell and garnish with croutons. Top with the pumpkin lid and serve.

Yield: 6 servings
Adapted from a recipe found on *SeedsofKnowledge.com*

Tarragon Chicken Salad Pitas

4   boneless skinless free-range chicken breasts (about 1¼ pounds),
    cooked, chopped
1   cup red seedless grapes, chopped
¾   cup low-fat plain yogurt
1   teaspoon tarragon
6   whole wheat pita breads
Lettuce leaves

Combine the chicken, grapes, yogurt, and tarragon in a bowl and mix
well. Refrigerate, covered, until chilled. Line pita breads with lettuce and
fill with the chicken mixture.

Yield: 6 servings
Adapted from a recipe found on SeedsofKnowledge.com

Buttermilk Herb Salad Dressing

⅔   cup buttermilk
2   tablespoons extra virgin olive oil
1   tablespoon fresh lemon juice
1   teaspoon Dijon mustard
½   teaspoon Celtic salt
¼   teaspoon freshly ground pepper
1   garlic clove, minced
2   tablespoons chopped chives
1   tablespoon chopped fresh thyme

Combine the buttermilk, olive oil, lemon juice, mustard, salt, pepper,
garlic, chives, and thyme in a small bowl. Whisk until blended.

Yield: about 1 cup
Adapted from a recipe found on SeedsofKnowledge.com

Minestrone

Cut or slice your choice of vegetables into bite-size pieces.

1   garlic clove, minced

1   tablespoon extra virgin olive oil

7   cups chopped vegetables such as cabbage, carrots, onion, green bell pepper, squash, corn

1   cup tomato sauce

5   cups low-sodium beef broth, or bouillon made with water and beef bouillon granules

16 ounces white beans, cooked

½   teaspoon oregano

½   teaspoon basil

½   teaspoon Celtic salt

¼   teaspoon pepper

⅓   cup uncooked small pasta of your choice

Freshly grated Parmesan cheese

Sauté the garlic briefly in the olive oil in a large pan over medium heat. Add the chopped vegetables. Sauté for about 5 minutes until vegetables begin to soften. Stir in the tomato sauce, beef broth, beans, oregano, basil, salt, and pepper. Simmer, uncovered, for 15 minutes. Sprinkle the pasta over the soup. Simmer for about 15 minutes longer or until pasta is tender. Serve in individual soup bowls. Sprinkle Parmesan cheese over each serving of soup.

Yield: 6 to 10 servings

Adapted from a recipe found on *SeedsofKnowledge*.com

Spicy Rice Soup

½ pound lean free-range ground beef

1 garlic clove, minced

3½ cups water

2 beef bouillon cubes

1 (10-ounce) can diced tomatoes with green chiles

½ cup niblet corn

½ cup green peas

¼ cup cooked whole grain rice

Green onion, chopped

Brown the ground beef with the garlic in a medium saucepan, stirring until crumbly; drain. Add the water, bouillon, tomatoes, corn, and peas; bring to a boil. Reduce heat and simmer, uncovered, for 5 minutes. Add rice and simmer, covered, for 5 minutes longer. Garnish with green onion and serve.

Yield: 4 servings

Adapted from a recipe found on *SeedsofKnowledge.com*

While fatty, whole milk is certainly not for adults, skim or nonfat milk may be. Researchers at Vanderbilt University found that skim milk seemed to lower the liver's output of LDL (bad) cholesterol. The calcium in skim milk may also have beneficial effects in high blood pressure and mild hypertension.

Leek and Potato Soup

2   large leeks, thinly sliced

6   medium potatoes, peeled, diced

4   cups low-sodium chicken broth

1   teaspoon Celtic salt

1   cup low-fat sour cream

2   cups skim milk

1   tablespoon chopped chives

Combine the leeks, potatoes, chicken broth, and salt in a large saucepan over medium-high heat. Bring to a boil. Reduce heat and simmer, covered, for 15 minutes or until potatoes are tender. Purée the potato mixture in blender and return it to the saucepan. Stir in the sour cream, milk, and chives. Heat gently.

Yield: 4 servings

Adapted from a recipe found on *SeedsofKnowledge.com*

Tuna Salad with Dill

Serve on a bed of lettuce leaves or use to fill sandwiches.

1   (6-ounce) can white tuna in water, drained, flaked

4   tablespoons low-fat yogurt

2   teaspoons fresh dill, chopped

3 or 4 chive leaves, chopped

¼   cup peeled, seeded cucumber, chopped

½   teaspoon grated lemon zest

Combine the tuna, yogurt, dill, chives, cucumber, and lemon zest in a bowl and mix well.

Yield: 2 servings

Adapted from a recipe found on *SeedsofKnowledge.com*

Cucumber and Sour Cream Salad Dressing

½   cucumber, peeled, seeded, grated (½ cup)

¼   teaspoon Celtic salt

2   teaspoons Dijon mustard

1   tablespoon vinegar or fresh lemon juice

Celtic Salt and freshly ground black pepper to taste

½   cup low-fat sour cream

¼   cup low-fat plain yogurt

1   tablespoon snipped fresh dill

Place the cucumber and the ¼ teaspoon salt in a small sieve set over a bowl; toss to combine. Drain for ten minutes. Combine the mustard, vinegar, and salt and pepper to taste in a blender and process for a few seconds. Add the sour cream, yogurt, and dill. Blend until smooth, scraping down the sides occasionally. Add the drained cucumber and blend just until combined.

Yield: 1½ cups

Adapted from a recipe found on *SeedsofKnowledge.com*

Bean and Pasta Soup

1½ cups water

2   (8-ounce) packages low-sodium instant vegetable broth mix

1   cup low-sodium canned stewed tomatoes

4½ ounces uncooked whole-grain small-shell macaroni

1   pound red kidney beans, cooked

1   cup chopped spinach

½   teaspoon oregano

½   teaspoon basil

¾   ounce fresh Parmesan cheese, grated

Combine the water and broth mix in a medium-sized saucepan over medium-high heat. Stir in the undrained tomatoes and bring to a boil. Add the macaroni. Reduce heat and simmer, uncovered, for 10 minutes. Stir in the beans, spinach, oregano, and basil; simmer for 10 minutes longer. Sprinkle Parmesan cheese over each serving of soup.

Yield: 4 servings

Adapted from a recipe found on *RecipeLand.com*

Wild Rice Soup

1   red bell pepper, chopped

1   green bell pepper, chopped

1   yellow bell pepper, chopped

1½ tablespoons red wine vinegar

4   tablespoons extra virgin olive oil

1   leek, chopped

1   medium carrot, sliced

1   rib celery, sliced

1½ cups cooked wild rice

1½ cups cooked white beans

6   cups low-sodium chicken broth

Celtic salt and freshly ground black pepper to taste

2   tablespoons finely chopped fresh oregano

2   tablespoons finely chopped fresh thyme

Combine the bell peppers and a mixture of the vinegar and olive oil in a bowl. Marinate in the refrigerator, covered, for 8 to 10 hours. Heat a small amount of olive oil in a saucepan over medium heat. Sauté the leek, carrot, and celery in the hot oil for about 3 minutes. Stir in the bell peppers, wild rice, beans, chicken broth, salt, and pepper. Reduce heat to low and simmer, uncovered, for about 20 minutes. Add the oregano and thyme, and cook for a few minutes longer. Serve hot.

Yield: 6 to 8 servings

BREAD, RICE,

& PASTA

I am the bread of life. Your fathers ate the manna in the wilderness, and are dead. This is the bread which comes down from heaven, that one may eat of it and not die. I am the living bread which came down from heaven. If anyone eats of this bread, he will live forever; and the bread that I shall give is My flesh, which I shall give for the life of the world. (John 6:48-51)

During the days of Jesus, bread was the staple food. In fact, Jesus taught us to pray in the Lord's Prayer, *give us this day our daily bread.* The two most common grains used in the Bible were whole grain wheat and barley. Whole grain breads contain the wheat germ, the bran, and the starch. In choosing breads today it is critically important that you choose whole grain breads like these in place of refined white bread. During the processing of whole grains to make white flour, approximately 80 percent of the nutrients are removed, and the high temperatures used in processing the grains create lipid peroxides, which in turn cause free radical reactions.

Sugars, partially hydrogenated fats, food additives, and food preservatives have been added to the processed white bread in order to prolong the shelf life and improve its flavor and texture. This low-fiber bread can become pastelike in the intestines, and lead to constipation as well as many GI diseases including diverticulosis, hemorrhoids, irritable bowel syndrome, and diverticulitis.

Once you make the change over to whole-grain breads, remember to store them in the refrigerator or freezer in order to prolong their shelf life, since they tend to go rancid much sooner because they contain essential fats.

When you choose pasta, select whole grain pasta and brown rice over the highly processed pastas and white rice.

Jesus knew that bread was the staple of man's physical life; in like manner, only those who accept Jesus as their atoning sacrifice and feed upon the Bread of Life will enjoy eternal, spiritual life.

Ezekiel's Bread

4 envelopes dry yeast

1 tablespoon honey

1 cup warm water

8 cups whole wheat flour

4 cups barley flour

2 cups soy flour

½ cup millet flour

¼ cup rye flour

1 cup mashed cooked lentils

4 to 5 tablespoons extra virgin olive oil

½ to ¾ cup honey

4 cups water

1 tablespoon Celtic salt

Stir the yeast and the 1 tablespoon honey into the 1 cup warm water and let stand for 10 minutes. Place the whole wheat flour, barley flour, soy flour, millet flour, and rye flour in a large bowl and stir to combine. Combine the lentils, olive oil, the ½ to ¾ cup honey, and ½ cup of the water in a blender; process until smooth. Combine the lentil mixture and the remaining 3½ cups water in a large bowl; stir until well mixed. Stir in 2 cups of the flour mixture. Stir in the yeast mixture. Add the salt and the remaining flour mixture. Knead until smooth on a floured board. Place in an oiled bowl. Let rise, covered, in a warm place until doubled in bulk. Knead again. Divide into 4 equal portions. Shape each portion into a large loaf. Place in greased loaf pans. Let rise, covered, in a warm place until doubled in bulk. Bake at 375 degrees for 45 minutes to 1 hour or until bread tests done.

Yield: 4 loaves

See pages 87-88 of *What Would Jesus Eat?* by Don Colbert

Apricot Couscous

1½ cups water

2   ounces dried apricots, finely chopped

1   teaspoon extra virgin olive oil

⅓ teaspoon cardamom

1   cup couscous

Combine the water, apricots, olive oil, and cardamom in a medium-sized saucepan over high heat. Cover and bring to a full boil. Remove from heat. Stir in the couscous. Let stand, covered, for 5 minutes or until liquid is absorbed.

Yield: 5 servings

Orzo Stuffing

Use to stuff poultry, or simply serve as a side dish.

2   (14-ounce) cans low-sodium chicken broth
16 ounces uncooked orzo (pasta)
1   tablespoon extra virgin olive oil
1   medium onion, chopped
1   large green bell pepper, seeded, diced
1   large red bell pepper, seeded, diced
1   teaspoon cumin

Place the chicken broth in a large saucepan over medium-high heat. Bring to a boil. Add the orzo and cook for 7 minutes; drain, and place in a large bowl. Heat the olive oil in a small skillet over medium-high heat. Sauté the onion and bell peppers in the hot oil for 5 minutes or until vegetables are soft. Add the cumin and sauté for 1 minute longer; remove from heat. Add the onion mixture to the orzo. Toss to combine.

Yield: 12 servings
Adapted from a recipe found on *Recipes.alastra.com*

Pasta with Sun-Dried Tomatoes

½   cup dry sun-dried tomatoes

1½ cups evaporated skim milk

1½ cups low-fat cottage cheese

1 or 2 garlic cloves, minced

½   teaspoon Celtic salt

½   teaspoon freshly ground black pepper

⅛   teaspoon hot red pepper flakes

¾   cup freshly grated Parmesan cheese

2   tablespoons extra virgin olive oil

16 ounces uncooked whole-grain pasta

¾   cup fresh basil leaves, chopped

Place the sun-dried tomatoes in a medium saucepan and add enough water to cover; place over medium-high heat and bring to a boil. Remove from heat. Let stand for 8 to 10 minutes. Drain, and discard the water. Chop the tomatoes. Combine the evaporated milk, cottage cheese, garlic, salt, black pepper, hot red pepper flakes, and Parmesan cheese in a food processor container and process until smooth. Add the olive oil and pulse until well blended. Pour the mixture into a saucepan and warm over low heat; do not boil. Cook the pasta in boiling water in a saucepan; drain. Place the hot pasta in a large serving bowl. Pour the cottage cheese mixture over the pasta and sprinkle with tomatoes and basil.

Yield: 8 servings

Adapted from a recipe found on *RecipeArchive.com*

Choose whole-grain products! Besides bread, you should be able to find whole-grain pasta, whole-grain muffins and bagels, and whole-grain pretzels. If the label on these products does not read "whole wheat" or "whole grain," you should assume that the product is made completely or partially with refined flour.

Refined White Flour

The processing of whole grains of wheat to white flour takes many steps. The wheat kernel is composed of an outer layer called the "bran," which is rich in B vitamins, minerals, and fiber. The next layer is the wheat germ, which is the sprouting portion of the kernel. The wheat germ is a rich source of vitamins B and E. The next layer is the endosperm, which is the starch or food supply for the sprouting seed. The endosperm makes up approximately 80 to 85 percent of the grain. The germ is about 3 percent, and the bran about 15 percent.

Refined white flour is pure endosperm or starch. Both the bran and the germ have been removed, along with approximately 80 percent of the wheat's nutrients. The endosperm has far lower B vitamin and mineral content than the germ and bran, and also significantly less fiber.

Not only have 80 percent of the nutrients been removed, but the milling process involves such high temperatures that the remaining grain is damaged by oxidation. Flour at the end of the refining process actually has a grayish appearance from the oxidation. That color, of course, would be offensive to most consumers. So a chemical agent such as chlorine dioxide, acetone peroxide, or benzoyl peroxide is used to bleach the flour to make it white. This bleaching process destroys even more of the few vitamins that remain. In addition, the bleaches can react with fatty acids to produce peroxides that are toxic and that can cause free-radical reactions. (Just compare these bleach products to the labels on chemical bleaches in your home such as Clorox!) In all, the milling and bleaching processes used today remove some twenty-two important nutrients from our bread, including fiber, vitamins, and minerals.

Butternut Pasta

4   shallots, chopped
1   large butternut squash, peeled, cut into ¼-inch cubes
18 ounces apple cider
3   tablespoons extra virgin olive oil
1   teaspoon nutmeg
Freshly ground black pepper to taste
16 ounces whole grain pasta
1   cup freshly grated Parmesan cheese

Heat a bit of olive oil in a large skillet over medium heat. Sauté the shallots in the hot oil for about 5 minutes or until soft. Add the squash and sauté for about 5 minutes. Slowly add the apple cider, olive oil, nutmeg, and pepper; bring to a boil. Reduce heat and simmer for about 20 minutes or until squash is very soft. Prepare the pasta in a kettle using the package directions. Drain the cooked pasta and return it to the kettle. Add the Parmesan cheese and all but 1 cup of the squash mixture; stir to combine. Serve individual servings of pasta, surrounded with steamed vegetables and topped with about a tablespoon of squash mixture.

Yield: 6 to 8 servings
Adapted from a recipe found on *Recipes.alastra.com*

Pasta with Olive Sauce

Schedule the cooking so the pasta is still hot

when the sauce is finished.

6   tablespoons extra virgin olive oil

1½ cups black olives, rinsed, pitted, chopped

5   sun-dried tomatoes packed in oil, drained, chopped

½   onion, finely chopped

2   garlic cloves, minced

¼   teaspoon hot red pepper flakes

1   teaspoon chopped fresh rosemary leaves

1   tablespoon chopped fresh marjoram leaves

4   tablespoons chopped fresh parsley

½   cup red wine

1 to 2 tablespoonsbottled capers, drained and rinsed

16 ounces whole grain pasta

Grated fresh Parmesan cheese

Combine 4 tablespoons of the olive oil, olives, sun-dried tomatoes, onion, garlic, red pepper flakes, rosemary, marjoram, and 2 tablespoons of the parsley in a saucepan over medium heat. Stir in 4 tablespoons of the olive oil, and sauté for about 5 minutes or until onion is softened. Stir in the wine and the capers. Simmer, uncovered, for about 5 minutes. Prepare the pasta using the package directions; drain and place in a serving bowl. Add the olive mixture, the remaining 4 tablespoons parsley, and the remaining 2 tablespoons olive oil. Toss to combine. Top with Parmesan cheese and serve.

Yield: 6 servings

Adapted from a recipe found on *Recipes.alastra.com*

Nutritionally Rich Barley Bread

While we do not know with certainty that Jesus ate wheat bread, we do know that He ate barley bread. In the story of the feeding of the five thousand men—plus women and children—the miracle occurred because Jesus broke, blessed, and multiplied five barley loaves and two small fish brought to the event by a young boy. Barley loaves were also multiplied by Elisha; he multiplied twenty loaves of barley bread to feed a hundred men (See 2 Kings 4:42-44).

Roman gladiators were sometimes called *hordearii*, which means "barley eaters," because the grain was added to their diet to give them bursts of strength before their contests. Barley is considered to be one of three balanced starches (rice and potatoes being the other two) that are rich in complex carbohydrates and fuel the body with a steady flow of energy.

In some areas of the Middle East, barley has been called the "medicine for the heart." It contains fiber that can lower the risk of heart disease by reducing artery-clogged LDL (bad) cholesterol. This same high fiber content keeps a person regular, relieving constipation and warding off a variety of digestive problems. It may also help block the development of cancer.

In a study conducted at Montana State University, a group of men ate a high-barley diet, including cereal, bread, cake, and muffins made from barley flour. After consuming three servings a day of this food for six weeks, the cholesterol levels of these men were an average of 15 percent lower. Those with the highest cholesterol levels at the start of the study showed the most significant improvement. Another group of men who ate the same products made with wheat or bran flour did not have a drop in their cholesterol counts.

Barley is available on the market today, but you do have to look for it. Barley bread is virtually nonexistent—you'd have to make it yourself from the grain you could find. The vast majority of barley grown today is used to feed livestock or to manufacture whiskey and beer. Barley grain is rarely eaten by itself; however, it is sometimes used as an ingredient in soups.

The Mediterranean Diet emphasizes unprocessed foods. Complex carbohydrates are at the base. These foods include brown rice or whole-grain rice, whole-grain pasta, and whole-grain bread—ideally, all should be prepared fresh daily without preservatives. Other grains appropriate for the base of this pyramid are bulgur wheat (cracked whole wheat), couscous, polenta (coarse corn meal), and potatoes. Whole-grain breads consumed in Mediterranean nations have a high amount of fiber without excessive sugars, hydrogenated fats, or food additives. In Mediterranean nations, whole grains are commonly consumed with each meal.

Whole Wheat Raisin Nut Bread

3   cups whole wheat flour

¼   cup wheat bran

¼   cup toasted wheat germ

2   teaspoons baking powder

1¼ teaspoons baking soda

1   teaspoon cinnamon

½   teaspoon Celtic salt

1½ cups buttermilk

½   cup honey

¼   cup extra virgin olive oil

¾   cup raisins

½   cup chopped walnuts or pecans

Place the flour, bran, wheat germ, baking powder, baking soda, cinnamon, and salt in a large bowl; stir to combine. Combine the buttermilk, honey, and olive oil in a medium bowl and whisk to combine. Add the buttermilk mixture to the flour mixture and blend well. Fold in the raisins and walnuts; mixture will be slightly stiff. Spoon into a well-greased 5x9x3-inch loaf pan. Bake at 350 degrees for about 1 hour or until wooden pick inserted in the center comes out clean. Cool in the pan for 10 minutes or until cool enough to handle. Remove to a wire rack to cool completely.

Yield: 1 loaf

Adapted from a recipe found on *CookbooksOnline.com*

Honey Rolled Wheat Bread

1   tablespoon plus 2 teaspoons dry yeast
2   cups milk, scalded, cooled
⅓   cup honey
¼   cup extra virgin olive oil
¼   cup wheat germ
1   tablespoon Celtic salt
5   cups whole wheat flour
1   cup rolled wheat or rolled oats

Dissolve the yeast in ¼ cup warm water in a small bowl. Mix the milk, honey, olive oil, wheat germ, and salt in a large bowl. Stir in the yeast mixture and 2 cups of the flour. Add the rolled wheat and enough of the remaining whole wheat flour to make dough. Knead on a floured surface until smooth and elastic. Place in a greased bowl, turning to coat the surface. Let rise, covered, in a warm place until doubled in bulk. Punch the dough down. Shape into 2 loaves in greased loaf pans. Let rise, covered, in a warm place until doubled in bulk. Bake at 375 degrees for 40 minutes or until breads test done.

Yield: 2 loaves

Adapted from a recipe found on *CookbooksOnline.com*

Wheat bran's high fiber content is one of the best-known dietary sources of insoluable fiber.

The nutritional breakdown of just one ounce of wheat bran is as follows:

Calories	60
Fiber	12 grams
Fat	1 gram
Potassium	410 milligrams
Carbohydrate	18 grams
Protein	5 grams

Sunflower Wheat Bread

2   cups whole wheat flour

½   cup wheat germ

1   tablespoon baking powder

1   teaspoon Celtic salt

1½ tablespoons poppy seeds

1   egg, room temperature

2   tablespoons extra virgin olive oil

2   tablespoons honey

1   cup skim milk, room temperature

1   cup plus 2 teaspoons raw hulled sunflower seeds

Spray a loaf pan with olive oil cooking spray; set aside. Preheat oven to 350 degrees. Combine the flour, wheat germ, baking powder, salt, and poppy seeds in a large bowl; mix well. Beat the egg lightly in a medium bowl; whisk in the olive oil, honey, oil and milk. Add to the flour mixture, stirring only until dry ingredients are moistened. Add 1 cup of the sunflower seeds, stirring until evenly distributed. Turn into a 4x8-inch loaf pan that has been sprayed with olive oil cooking spray. Smooth top, and sprinkle with 2 teaspoons sunflower seeds. Bake at 350 degrees for 60 to 70 minutes or until a wooden pick inserted in the center comes out clean. Cool in the pan for 10 minutes. Remove to a wire rack to cool completely.

Yield: 1 loaf

Adapted from a recipe found on *CookbooksOnline.com*

Buttered Beans with Basil

2   cups fresh green beans, cut into 2-inch pieces
2   tablespoons chopped onion
2   tablespoons chopped celery
¼   cup water
1   tablespoon extra virgin olive oil
1½ tablespoons minced fresh basil, or ½ teaspoon dried
¼   teaspoon Celtic salt
⅛   teaspoon freshly ground pepper

Combine the green beans, onion, celery, and water in a saucepan over medium heat. Cook, covered, for 5 to 10 minutes or until beans are tender. Drain. Stir in the olive oil, basil, salt, and pepper.

Yield: 3 or 4 servings

The breads of Jesus' time were coarse whole-grain breads, which were darker and heavier than the breads we have today. Since they were made with whole grain, including the bran and wheat germ, they had a much higher concentration of naturally occurring polyunsaturated oils.

Pumpkin Banana Bread

½   cup extra virgin olive oil

¾   cup sugar (or ¾ teaspoon liquid Stevia)

¾   cup packed brown sugar

4   eggs

1½ cups mashed ripe bananas

1½ cups canned or puréed pumpkin

1½ cups plain or vanilla-flavored yogurt

4   cups whole wheat flour

2   teaspoons baking powder

2   teaspoons baking soda

½   teaspoon Celtic salt

2   teaspoons cinnamon

1   teaspoon ginger

1½ teaspoons nutmeg

Combine the olive oil, sugars, eggs, bananas, pumpkin, and yogurt in a large mixing bowl and beat until smooth. Slowly add a mixture of the flour, baking powder, baking soda, salt, cinnamon, ginger, and nutmeg to the liquid mixture, mixing until well blended. Pour the mixture into two lightly greased and floured loaf pans. Bake at 350 degrees for 45 minutes or until golden brown and a wooden toothpick inserted in the center comes out clean.

Yield: 2 loaves

Adapted from a recipe found on *FabulousFoods.com*

Matzoh Balls

Place the drained cooked matzoh balls in simmering chicken soup or vegetable soup and simmer for about five minutes before serving.

4   eggs

¼   cup low-sodium chicken broth

¼   cup extra virgin olive oil

1½ teaspoons Celtic salt

Freshly ground pepper to taste

1   tablespoon chopped fresh parsley

1   cup matzoh meal

8   cups cold water

1   chicken bullion cube

Whisk the eggs and chicken broth together in a medium bowl. Slowly stir in the olive oil, salt, pepper, parsley, and matzoh meal. Chill, covered, for about one hour or until thickened. Combine the water and bullion cube in a saucepan over medium-high heat. Bring to a boil; reduce to a simmer. Shape the matzoh dough into 1-inch balls and drop into the simmering bouillon. Cook, covered, for 1 hour; drain.

Yield: 8 to 10
Adapted from a recipe found on *FabulousFoods.com*

Steamed Wheat

1   cup unroasted buckwheat groats

2   cups low-sodium chicken broth

1   teaspoon extra virgin olive oil

Celtic salt to taste

Toast the buckwheat in a small pan over medium heat for a few minutes until the color turns a bit darker; remove from heat. Combine the chicken broth, olive oil, and salt in a saucepan; bring to a boil. Add the toasted buckwheat slowly to the boiling broth mixture, stirring constantly. Reduce the heat and cook, covered, for 8 to 10 minutes or until liquid is nearly gone. Remove from heat. Let stand, covered, for 10 minutes longer. Serve hot.

Yield: 3 or 4 servings

Creamy Oat Porridge
**Set up the slow cooker before you go to bed,
and wake up to hot, creamy porridge.**

1   cup oat groats

4   cups water

Pinch of Celtic salt

Combine the groats, water, and salt in a slow cooker. Cook on Low for 8 to 10 hours. Serve warm with honey, molasses, or fresh fruit toppings.

Yield: 4 servings

Milk and Honey Bread

½ cup honey

1 cup skim milk

3 tablespoons extra virgin olive oil

1½ cups whole wheat flour

½ cup sugar (or ½ teaspoon liquid Stevia)

1 tablespoon baking powder

1 teaspoon Celtic salt

¾ cup chopped pecans

1 egg, beaten

Combine the honey and milk in a medium saucepan over medium heat and cook, stirring constantly, until honey dissolves. Stir in the olive oil. Remove from heat and let cool. Sift the flour, sugar, baking powder, and salt into a large mixing bowl. Add the pecans and toss to coat. Whisk the egg into the cooled milk mixture. Add the egg mixture to the flour mixture. Beat just until blended. Pour into a lightly greased and floured loaf pan and smooth top. Bake at 350 degrees for 65 to 75 minutes or until a wooden pick inserted in the center comes out clean. Cool in the pan on a wire rack for 10 minutes. Remove from the pan and cool completely on the rack.

Yield: 1 loaf

Adapted from a recipe found on *SeedsofKnowledge.com*

The calcium in milk builds bones in children and may help prevent or slow the development of osteoporosis in older women.

Just one cup of milk has these minerals:

Calcium	250 milligrams
Protein	8.4 grams
Potassium	406 milligrams
Sodium	126 milligrams

Applesauce Date Nut Bread

¾ cup chopped walnuts

1 cup chopped dates or raisins

1½ teaspoons baking soda

½ teaspoon Celtic salt

1 cup applesauce

3 tablespoons extra virgin olive oil

1½ cups whole wheat flour

1 cup sugar

2 eggs

1 teaspoon vanilla extract

Combine the walnuts, dates, baking soda, salt, applesauce, and olive oil in a large bowl and mix well; let stand for 20 minutes. Add the flour, sugar, eggs, and vanilla; mix well. Pour the batter into a lightly greased 9x5-inch loaf pan. Bake at 350 degrees for 1 hour or until a knife inserted in the center comes out clean. Cool in the pan on a wire rack for 10 minutes. Remove from the pan and cool completely on the rack.

Yield: 1 loaf

Adapted from a recipe found on *SeedsofKnowledge.com*

A word of warning—raisins have a much higher concentration of sugar than does other fresh fruit. They are also more subject to pesticide residue. To avoid problems I recommend that you choose organic raisins.

Cinnamon Bread with Apple Spread

2   cups whole wheat flour

1   cup sugar

4   teaspoons baking powder

1½ teaspoons cinnamon

½   teaspoon Celtic salt

1   cup buttermilk

⅓   cup extra virgin olive oil

2   teaspoons vanilla extract

2   eggs

Grease and flour the bottom of a 5x7-inch loaf pan. Combine the flour, sugar, baking powder, cinnamon, salt, buttermilk, olive oil, vanilla, and eggs in a large mixing bowl; beat for 3 minutes at medium speed. Pour the batter into the prepared loaf pan. Bake at 350 degrees for 45 to 55 minutes or until a wooden tooth pick inserted in the center comes out clean. Cool in the pan on a wire rack for 15 minutes. Remove from the pan and cool completely on the rack. Serve warm with Apple Spread.

Yield: 1 loaf

Apple Spread

8   ounces low-fat cream cheese, softened

⅔   cup finely chopped peeled apple

1   tablespoon confectioners' sugar

1   tablespoon milk

¼   teaspoon cinnamon

Combine the cream cheese, apple, confectioners' sugar, milk, and cinnamon in a blender or food processor container. Process until well mixed, scraping down the side occasionally.

Yield: 1 1/2 cups

Adapted from a recipe found on *SeedsofKnowledge.com*

Orange Juice Muffins

2 cups buttermilk baking mix

4 tablespoons sugar (or ⅓ teaspoon Stevia)

1 egg

1 teaspoon grated orange zest

⅓ cup orange juice

1 teaspoon cinnamon

Preheat the oven to 400 degrees. Grease bottoms only of 12 medium muffin cups. Combine the baking mix, half the sugar, egg, orange zest, and orange juice in a mixing bowl. Beat vigorously for 30 seconds. Fill the prepared muffin cups about ⅔ full. Mix the remaining sugar and the cinnamon together; sprinkle each muffin with about ½ teaspoon of the sugar mixture. Bake for 15 minutes or until muffins test done. Serve with honey.

Yield: 1 dozen
Adapted from a recipe found on *SeedsofKnowledge.com*

Nuts have been associated with cancer prevention, a lower risk of heart disease, and help for diabetes.

Banana Poppy Seed Muffins

2   medium bananas, peeled

1   egg

¾   cup sugar (or ¾ teaspoon Stevia)

¼   cup extra virgin olive oil

2   teaspoons grated orange zest

2   cups whole wheat flour

1½ tablespoons poppy seeds

2   teaspoons baking powder

½   teaspoon Celtic salt

Process the bananas in a blender to make 1 cup of banana purée. Combine the banana purée, egg, sugar, olive oil, and orange zest in a medium bowl; mix well. Place the flour, poppy seeds, baking powder, and salt in a large bowl and stir to combine. Stir the banana mixture into the flour mixture until evenly moistened. Spoon the batter into greased 2½-inch muffin cups. Bake at 375 degrees for 20 minutes or until a wooden toothpick inserted in the center comes out clean. Remove to a wire rack to cool.

Yield: 12 muffins

Adapted from a recipe found on *SeedsofKnowledge.com*

Apple Coffeecake Muffins

A sweet apple filling is a delicious surprise in these muffins.

1 small unpeeled apple, finely chopped

¼ cup chopped walnuts

2 tablespoons extra virgin olive oil

1 tablespoon sugar (or 6 to 9 drops Stevia)

1 teaspoon cinnamon

1½ cups 100% bran cereal

1½ cups skim milk

1 egg

½ cup packed brown sugar

⅓ cup extra virgin olive oil

2 cups whole wheat flour

1 tablespoon baking powder

1 teaspoon allspice

½ teaspoon Celtic salt

Grease large muffin cups or line with paper baking cups. Combine the apple, walnuts, the 2 tablespoons olive oil, sugar, and cinnamon in a small bowl and set aside. Combine the cereal and milk in a medium bowl; let stand for 5 minutes. Stir the egg, brown sugar, and the ⅓ cup olive oil into the cereal mixture. Place the flour, baking powder, allspice, and Celtic salt in a large bowl and stir to combine. Add the cereal mixture to the flour mixture, stirring just until moistened. Spoon half the batter into the prepared muffin cups. Gently press 1 tablespoon of the apple mixture into each partially filled muffin cup. Spoon the remaining batter over the tops of the muffins. Bake at 400 degrees for about 20 minutes or until firm to the touch. Cool in pans 5 minutes; remove to a wire rack to cool completely. Store in an airtight container.

Yield: 12 large muffins

Adapted from a recipe found on *SeedsofKnowledge.com*

Herb Onion Bread

3¼ cups whole wheat flour
2   envelopes dry yeast
2   tablespoons sugar (or 12 to 18 drops Stevia)
1   teaspoon Celtic salt
½   teaspoon sage
½   teaspoon crushed rosemary leaves
¼   teaspoon thyme
1   cup finely chopped onion
¼   cup extra virgin olive oil
1¼ cups warm water
1   egg

Combine 1½ cups of the flour, yeast, sugar, salt, sage, rosemary, and thyme in a large mixing bowl; mix well. Sauté the onion in hot olive oil in a saucepan for 5 minutes or until golden; add to the flour mixture. Add the water and egg to the flour mixture and blend at low speed until moistened. Beat at medium speed for 3 minutes longer. Gradually stir in the remaining flour by hand to make a stiff batter. Spoon the batter into a greased 2-quart baking dish. Let rise, covered, in a warm place until light and doubled in bulk. Bake at 375 degrees for 35 to 40 minutes or until golden brown. Remove from pan to a wire rack to cool.

Yield: 1 loaf
Adapted from a recipe found on *SeedsofKnowledge.com*

Cornmeal Muffins

1½ cups whole wheat flour

½ cup yellow cornmeal

¼ cup sugar (or ¼ teaspoon Stevia)

1 tablespoon baking powder

¾ teaspoon Celtic salt

½ cup small curd cottage cheese

¾ cup skim milk

¼ cup extra virgin olive oil

1 egg

½ cup grated fresh Parmesan cheese

½ teaspoon thyme

Combine the flour, cornmeal, sugar, baking powder, and salt in a large mixing bowl. Place the cottage cheese in a medium bowl and mash with a fork. Add the milk, olive oil, and egg to the cottage cheese and mix well. Add the cottage cheese mixture to the flour mixture, and stir just until moistened. Fold in the Parmesan cheese and thyme. Fill greased or paper-lined muffin cups ¾ full. Bake at 400 degrees for 20 to 25 minutes or until muffins test done. Remove to a wire rack to cool.

Yield: 12 muffins

Adapted from a recipe found on *SeedsofKnowledge.com*

Basil Tomato Bread with Scallion Spread

2   cups whole wheat flour

1   teaspoon baking soda

1   tablespoon baking powder

1   teaspoon Celtic salt

1   small piece of gingerroot

½   cup chopped fresh basil leaves, or ¼ cup dried

1   scallion, cut in 1-inch pieces

3   tomatoes, seeded, quartered

1   tablespoon tomato paste

1¼ cups sugar (or 1¼ teaspoons Stevia)

3   eggs

½   cup extra virgin olive oil

Scallion Spread

Combine the flour, baking soda, baking powder, and salt in a food processor container and process for 2 seconds; remove the flour mixture to a bowl and set aside. Place the gingerroot, basil, and scallion in the food processor and process for 2 seconds. Add the tomatoes and tomato paste; process for 10 seconds until puréed. Add the sugar and process for 30 seconds. Add the eggs and process for 1 minute. Add the olive oil and process briefly until blended. Add the flour mixture and pulse five or six times until the flour has disappeared. Spread the dough in a greased loaf pan. Bake at 350 degrees for 40 minutes or until bread tests done. Serve with Scallion Spread.

Scallion Spread

8 ounces low-fat cream cheese, softened, cut into 4 pieces

1 large scallion cut into 1-inch pieces, or 1 bunch chives

⅛ teaspoon Tabasco sauce

Combine the cream cheese, scallion, and Tabasco in a food processor container and process until well mixed.

Yield: ¾ cup

Adapted from a recipe found on SeedsofKnowledge.com

Peach Bread

1 (29-ounce) can sliced peaches, drained

¼ cup extra virgin olive oil

1 egg

¼ cup low-fat sour cream

3 cups whole wheat flour

1 tablespoon baking powder

¾ cup sugar (or ¾ teaspoon stevia)

¼ teaspoon Celtic salt

½ teaspoon allspice

¼ cup finely chopped walnuts

¼ cup packed brown sugar

Reserve five of the peach slices for the topping and purée the remainder in a blender or food processor. Add the olive oil, egg, and sour cream, and process until blended. Combine the flour, baking powder, sugar, salt, and allspice in a deep bowl and mix lightly. Add the peach mixture to the dry ingredients, and mix just until moistened. Pour into a greased loaf pan. Mix the walnuts and brown sugar together; sprinkle over top of dough.

Arrange peach slices over the sugar mixture. Bake at 350 degrees for 50 minutes or until bread tests done.

Yield: 1 loaf
Adapted from a recipe found on SeedsofKnowledge.com

Thyme Biscuits

2   cups whole wheat flour
3   teaspoons baking powder
1   teaspoon minced fresh thyme
½   teaspoon minced fresh parsley
½   teaspoon minced fresh rosemary
½   cup grated Parmesan cheese
5   tablespoons extra virgin olive oil
½   cup skim milk

Preheat the oven to 400 degrees. Place the flour, baking powder, thyme, parsley, rosemary, and Parmesan cheese in a large mixing bowl, and use a fork to stir and combine. Slowly stir in the olive oil; mixture will be crumbly. Add the milk and stir until dough holds together; you may add more milk if necessary. Drop by large spoonfuls 1 inch apart onto a greased baking sheet. Bake for 10 to 12 minutes.

Yield: 10 to 12 biscuits
Adapted from a recipe found on SeedsofKnowledge.com

Raisin and Honey Bread

1¾ cups plain low-fat yogurt

2   egg whites

2¼ cups whole wheat flour

1½ teaspoons baking powder

½   teaspoon baking soda

½   teaspoon Celtic salt

½   cup raisins

2   tablespoons fresh honey

Preheat the oven to 425 degrees. Combine the yogurt and egg whites in a large bowl and mix well. Place the flour, baking powder, baking soda, and salt in a medium bowl and stir to combine. Slowly stir the flour mixture into the yogurt mixture. Add the raisins and honey and stir well. Spoon the dough into a loaf pan that has been lightly coated with olive oil. Bake for 20 minutes or until the top is brown.

Yield: 1 loaf

During His stay in the wilderness, Jesus had been fasting, and He was extremely hungry. It is no surprise that satan would come to tempt Jesus with food that He craved the most to quench His hunger, the food that was the foremost staple of His diet: bread.

Tabouleh

1   cup cracked wheat
1   cup fresh parsley leaves, chopped
½   cup fresh mint leaves, chopped
½   cup onion, minced
½   cup scallions (green tops only), chopped
½   cup extra virgin olive oil
¼   cup fresh lemon juice
1   medium tomato, coarsely chopped
Celtic salt and freshly ground pepper to taste

Place the cracked wheat in a bowl and add enough warm water to cover; let stand for 1 hour (it will expand greatly). Drain, and press out excess water. Place the soaked wheat, parsley, mint, onion, scallions, olive oil, lemon juice, tomato, salt, and pepper in a bowl and toss to combine. Chill, covered, for at least 1 hour. Serve over lettuce.

Yield: 6 servings
Adapted from a recipe found on *CookbooksOnline.com*

Tahini Dressing

1   cup plain yogurt
½   cup tahini
Fresh lemon juice to taste
Minced garlic to taste
Celtic salt and pepper to taste

Combine the yogurt, tahini, lemon juice, garlic, salt, and pepper in a bowl and whisk to blend.

Adapted from a recipe found on *CookbooksOnline.com*

Falafel

4 cups cooked garbanzo beans, partially drained, mashed

⅓ cup bread crumbs

¼ teaspoon each basil, thyme, marjoram, cumin, turmeric

1 tablespoon fresh or dried parsley, chopped

Celtic salt and black pepper to taste

3 tablespoons tahini

1 hot red chile pepper, chopped

1 to 3 garlic cloves, minced

1 to 3 eggs

½ cup whole wheat flour

4 tablespoons extra virgin olive oil

Tahini Dressing

Combine the garbanzo beans, bread crumbs, basil, thyme, marjoram, cumin, turmeric, parsley, salt, black pepper, tahini, chile pepper, and garlic in a large bowl; mix lightly. Mix in the eggs, 1 at a time; mixture will have a semisoft consistency. Shape garbanzo mixture into 1-inch balls or small patties and roll in flour to coat. Brown in olive oil in a heavy skillet over medium heat. Drain on paper towels. Serve in pita bread with yogurt, chopped tomatoes, lettuce or sprouts, shredded cheese, and Italian or Tahini Dressing.

Yield: 8 to 10 servings

MEAT

DISHES

". . . bring the fatted calf here and kill it, and let us eat and be merry." (Luke 15:23)

A staple item in the diet of most Americans is red meat. With fast-food restaurants on nearly every corner, each person in this country eats an average of three hamburgers every week and about seventy pounds of red meat per year! In the days of Jesus, red meat was primarily reserved for feasts, weddings, holidays, banquets, and parties. In the Bible story of the prodigal son, when the long-lost son returned home, his father celebrated by killing the "fatted calf"—that's because the fatted calf was reserved for special occasions. Beef was actually considered a luxury and was consumed by the more affluent people.

Fish was the most common protein source in the days of Jesus. It was an inexpensive and regular part of the average person's diet. Unfortunately, much of the fish consumed in modern America is fried, which actually cancels out the beneficial health-promoting effects of the fish oils. Also, most fish served in restaurants is "unclean" fish, in the form of catfish or shell fish. These are bottom feeders, which actually harbor toxins and disease-causing microorganisms.

Jesus and His disciples did not eat pork, since it was an "unclean" meat. When people did eat meat, it was usually young lamb or goat. These tender and more plentiful animals grazed in open pastures, and were what we would call "range-fed" in modern day. Range-fed meat also does not contain an overabundance of pesticides, antibiotics, steroids or growth hormones that may be fed to animals.

In the time of Jesus, people grilled, baked, or stewed meat instead of frying it, and they added fresh herbs, onions, and garlic to impart a robust flavor. They marinated meat in wine or yogurt to tenderize it and to improve its flavor, and could sprinkle or grate a small amount of feta cheese over it to impart even more flavor. Remember, though, that

Jesus would probably only have eaten small portions of meat—about two to four ounces per serving.

Eat meat very slowly, and chew each bite approximately twenty to thirty times in order to improve digestion and assimilation. I tell patients to set the fork down between each bite of meat and do not consume excessive amounts of a beverage with a meal. Most Americans will chew their meat a few times and then wash it down with a soft drink or iced tea. This is one of the reasons why we have an epidemic of heartburn and indigestion. Simply relax, slow down, make dining an experience, place the fork down between each bite, and chew each bite thoroughly.

If red meat is to be eaten, I strongly recommend that my patients and clients do the following:

1. *Cut down on the intake of animal protein. Eat fewer portions of red meat per month.*

2. *Make sure all the red meat you eat is trimmed of fat. Choose "extra lean" and "range-fed" meats. If possible choose kosher meat.*

3. *Store meat in the coldest part of the refrigerator, and use it within two to five days of purchase. Ground beef and sausage should be thrown out after two days. Frozen meats should be defrosted either in a refrigerator or microwave oven.*

4. *Cooked meats should not be left outside the refrigerator for longer than two hours. If food is left out even for a few hours, the bacteria multiplies rapidly. Reheat all food containing meat to at least 160 degrees.*

Lebanese Chicken

¾ cup fresh lemon juice

8 garlic cloves, minced

2 tablespoons minced fresh thyme, or 2 teaspoons dried

1 tablespoon paprika

1½ teaspoons cumin

¾ teaspoon cayenne pepper

6 pounds skinless free-range chicken pieces

Combine the lemon juice, garlic, thyme, paprika, cumin, and cayenne in a small bowl and whisk well. Arrange the chicken in a 9x13x2-inch glass baking dish. Pour the marinade over the chicken; turn chicken to coat. Marinate, covered, in the refrigerator for 8 to 10 hours, turning occasionally. Combine the chicken and marinade in a large roasting pan and season with salt and pepper. Bake at 425 degrees for about 50 minutes or until chicken is brown and cooked through, turning occasionally.

Yield: 4 to 6 servings
Adapted from a recipe found on *RecipeSource.com*

It is very likely that Jesus ate beef since we know that many people celebrated His presence in their homes, and we also know from Scripture that He attended weddings, where beef was often included as a feast food. Beef consumption would not have been a daily or even a weekly practice for Jesus.

Rolled Stuffed Grape Leaves

If you can find fresh grape leaves, you may substitute them for those that come in a jar. Dip fresh grape leaves in boiling water for about 30 seconds before using.

2   pounds lean ground free-range lamb or beef

¾   cup uncooked long grain rice

Celtic salt and pepper to taste

⅛   teaspoon cinnamon

1   (16-ounce) jar grape leaves

1   cup water

3   garlic cloves, minced

3   tablespoons fresh mint, chopped

Juice of 2 or 3 limes

Combine the ground lamb, rice, salt, pepper, and cinnamon in a bowl and mix well. Remove the stem from each grape leaf and spread the leaves on a flat surface. Spoon 1 teaspoonful lamb mixture in the center of each leaf about ½ inch from the stem point. Fold leaf forward toward the filling; then fold one side over and roll leaf forward very tightly. When fully rolled, squeeze to secure. Place the stuffed leaves in layers in a Dutch oven or heavy kettle. Combine the water, garlic, mint, and lime juice in a bowl and mix well. Drizzle the lime juice mixture over the stuffed grape leaves. Cover and bring to a boil over high heat. Reduce heat and cook, covered, very slowly for 1 hour, or until grape leaves are steamed soft and cut easily with a fork; add more water while cooking if necessary. Do not overcook or the leaves will fall apart.

Yield: 8 to 12 servings

Adapted from a recipe found on *RecipeSource.com*

Lamb Stew

4   free-range lamb shoulders

2   medium carrots, sliced

2   medium ribs celery, sliced

1   medium onion, sliced

4   medium potatoes, sliced

1   (14-ounce) can low-sodium chicken broth

1½ cups water

Celtic salt and pepper to taste

Marjoram leaves

Place the lamb in a shallow baking pan. Arrange the carrots, celery, onion, and potatoes around the lamb in the pan. Add the chicken broth and water. Season with salt, pepper, and marjoram. Roast at 400 to 425 degrees for 40 to 45 minutes or until done to taste.

Yield: 4 servings

Adapted from a recipe found on *CookbooksOnline.com*

When purchasing a fresh fish look at the eyes. They should be shiny and bright, bulging, firm, and clear. Then look at the scales—they should be shiny. Touch the fish. If you can make a dent in the flesh, don't buy it. The flesh should spring back to the touch. The gills of the fish should be firm and pink. Finally, if it smells "fishy" don't buy it. Fresh fish has almost no odor.

Rosemary Chicken Stew

2   medium potatoes, peeled, cut into small cubes
3   tablespoons extra virgin olive oil
1   onion, finely chopped
2   garlic cloves, minced
1   pound boneless skinless free-range chicken pieces
3   carrots, peeled, cut in ½-inch pieces
Juice of ½ lemon
2   tablespoons fresh rosemary, or 1 tablespoon dried
2   tablespoons fresh basil, or 1 tablespoon dried
½   cup parsley, chopped
12 to 14 pitted black olives, sliced

Combine the potatoes with enough water to cover in a saucepan and bring to a boil. Boil for about 5 to 10 minutes or until tender; drain. Heat the olive oil in a medium saucepan over medium heat. Sauté the onion and garlic in the oil for about 5 minutes. Add the chicken and cook for about 5 minutes. Add 1½ cups water, carrots, lemon juice, rosemary, basil, parsley, and olives. Simmer, uncovered, for about 30 minutes or until chicken is cooked through.

Yield: 4 servings
Adapted from a recipe found on *RecipeSource.com*

Lebanese Cabbage Rolls

1   cup dry whole-grain rice, cooked

1   pound coarsely ground free-range beef

2   cups canned tomatoes, or 1 (6-ounce) can tomato paste

2   teaspoons Celtic salt

½   teaspoon pepper

½   teaspoon allspice

1   head cabbage

3   garlic cloves

Juice of 2 limes

Place the rice, ground beef, and half the tomatoes or half the tomato paste in a bowl. Add 1½ teaspoons salt, pepper, and allspice; mix well. Place several cups of water and a pinch of Celtic salt in a saucepan and bring to a boil. Separate the cabbage leaves. Drop several leaves at a time in the boiling salted water. Cook for about 5 minutes or until limp; drain. Trim off heavy stems. Arrange stems in the bottom of a heavy saucepan or Dutch oven. Place 1 heaping tablespoon ground beef mixture in the center of each leaf until all beef mixture is used; roll firmly. Arrange the cabbage rolls in neat rows in the stem-lined saucepan, making several layers, and placing garlic cloves among the rolls. Add the remaining tomatoes and enough hot water to cover the rolls. Sprinkle ½ teaspoon salt over the top. Simmer, covered, for 45 minutes to 1 hour or until beef is well cooked. Add the lime juice during the last 15 minutes of cooking.

Yield: 8 to 10 servings

Adapted from a recipe found on *CookbooksOnline.com*

Mediterranean Fish Stew

Haddock, sole, and perch are especially good selections for this stew.

2 tablespoons extra virgin olive oil

½ cup diced onions

1 garlic clove, minced

1 (16-ounce) can stewed tomatoes

2 carrots, peeled, sliced

1 tablespoon low-sodium chicken bouillon granules

½ teaspoon marjoram

1 bay leaf

Dash of freshly ground black pepper

1½ cups water

2 tablespoons whole-grain flour

1 pound fresh fish fillets, cut into large chunks

4 mushrooms, sliced

½ green bell pepper, cut into 1-inch pieces

Heat the olive oil in a medium saucepan over medium-high heat. Sauté the onions and garlic in the hot oil for 3 minutes. Stir in the undrained tomatoes, carrots, bouillon, marjoram, bay leaf, and black pepper. Combine the water and flour in a small bowl and whisk well. Stir the flour mixture into the tomato mixture. Simmer, covered, for 30 minutes or until carrots are tender. Remove the bay leaf. Stir in the fish, mushrooms, and bell pepper. Cook, covered, for 5 minutes or until fish flakes with a fork. Serve immediately.

Yield: 4 servings.
Adapted from a recipe found on *CookbooksOnline.com*

Broiled Lamb

**Serve these lamb chops and vegetables
over whole-grain pasta if desired.**

4 to 6 lean free-range lamb chops

Celtic salt and freshly ground pepper

2   tablespoons extra virgin olive oil

3   medium zucchini, sliced

1   onion, coarsely chopped

1   red or green bell pepper, sliced

1   garlic clove, minced

1   teaspoon basil

¼   teaspoon marjoram

Preheat the broiler for about 5 minutes. Broil the lamb on one side 6 inches from the heat source for 5 minutes; season with salt and pepper. Turn and broil for 5 minutes longer; season with salt and pepper once again. Heat the olive oil in a large skillet over medium-low heat. Sauté the zucchini, onion, bell pepper, and garlic in the hot oil for about 5 minutes or until tender-crisp. Sprinkle the basil, marjoram, and ½ teaspoon Celtic salt over the vegetables. Cook, covered, for 4 more minutes or until vegetables are tender.

Yield: 4 to 6 servings

Adapted from a recipe found on *CookbooksOnline.com*

Sole Mediterranean

1   (16-ounce) can stewed tomatoes
½   cup onion, chopped
¼   cup green bell pepper, chopped
¾   teaspoon garlic salt
½   teaspoon oregano
2   tablespoons extra virgin olive oil
1   small eggplant, peeled, sliced
1   pound fresh sole fillets
2   tablespoons cold water
1   tablespoon cornstarch
½   cup freshly grated Parmesan cheese

Combine the undrained tomatoes, onion, bell pepper, garlic salt, and oregano in a medium saucepan over medium-high heat. Bring to boil. Reduce heat and simmer, uncovered, for 15 minutes, stirring occasionally. Heat the olive oil in a large skillet, brown the eggplant in the hot oil. Drain on paper towels. Arrange the eggplant in a 7x12-inch baking dish. Arrange the fish over the eggplant layer. Whisk the water and cornstarch together. Stir the cornstarch mixture into the tomato mixture. Cook, uncovered, over medium-low heat until thick and bubbly, stirring constantly. Pour the hot tomato mixture evenly over the fish layer. Bake, tightly covered with foil, at 350 degrees for 30 minutes. Sprinkle with Parmesan cheese. Bake, uncovered, for 2 to 3 minutes longer.

Yield: 4 servings
Adapted from a recipe found on *CookbooksOnline.com*

Mediterranean Chicken and Mushrooms

3 pounds free-range chicken pieces, skinned

¼ cup whole wheat flour

4 tablespoons extra virgin olive oil

1 cup chopped onions

1 cup chopped green bell peppers

1 garlic clove, minced

8 ounces fresh mushrooms, sliced (Two 4-ounce cans of sliced mushrooms, drained, may be substituted for the fresh mushrooms.)

1 (28-ounce) can whole tomatoes, broken up

1 cup water

1¼ teaspoons Celtic salt

1 teaspoon Italian dressing mix

Pinch of ground red pepper

1 cup uncooked whole-grain rice

Coat the chicken with flour and shake off excess. Heat the olive oil in large heavy skillet over medium heat. Brown the chicken well, a few pieces at a time, in the hot oil. Remove chicken from skillet. Sauté the onions, bell peppers, and garlic in the oil remaining in the skillet for 3 minutes. Add the mushrooms to the onion mixture and sauté for 5 minutes longer. Stir in the undrained tomatoes, water, salt, Italian dressing mix, and red pepper. Bring to a boil. Stir in the rice. Return the chicken to the skillet. Reduce heat and simmer, covered, for 20 minutes or until chicken is tender and liquid is absorbed.

Yield: 4 servings

Adapted from a recipe found on *CookbooksOnline.com*

Greek Meatballs with Mushroom sauce

2   pounds free-range extra-lean ground beef
4   sprigs of parsley, chopped
2   medium onions, chopped
2   slices whole grain bread, crusts trimmed
Worcestershire sauce
Oregano
Garlic Powder
Celtic salt and pepper to taste
Extra virgin olive oil
Mushroom Sauce

Combine the ground beef, parsley, and onions in a bowl; mix well. Sprinkle the bread with enough water to moisten; tear into small pieces and add to the beef mixture. Sprinkle the beef mixture liberally with Worcestershire sauce and oregano; sprinkle lightly with garlic powder. Season with salt and pepper and mix well. Chill, covered, for at least 2 hours. Shape into 1-inch balls. Arrange the meatballs in a foil-lined rectangular baking dish coated with olive oil. Bake at 350 degrees, uncovered, until brown on all sides and cooked through, stirring occasionally. Drain, reserving 3 tablespoons of the drippings. Serve with Mushroom Sauce.

Yield: 8 servings

Mushroom Sauce

2   Bermuda onions
3   green bell peppers
3   tablespoons beef drippings
2   tablespoons extra virgin olive oil

Worcestershire sauce to taste

Oregano to taste

Celtic salt and pepper to taste

1   cup sliced fresh mushrooms

1   (8-ounce) can tomato sauce

Slice the onions and bell peppers into thin rings. Combine the beef drippings, olive oil, onions, and bell peppers in a heavy skillet over medium
heat. Season with Worcestershire sauce, oregano, salt, and pepper. Cook,
covered, over low heat for 10 minutes. Add the mushrooms and cook,
covered, for 5 to 10 minutes longer or until vegetables are soft. Stir in the
tomato sauce. Adjust the seasonings and cook, covered, for 15 minutes
longer. Stir in the meatballs and cook for 15 to 20 minutes over low heat.
Serve over brown rice.

Adapted from a recipe found on *CookbooksOnline*.com

Turkey Tarragon Pitas

½ cup low-fat lemon yogurt
1 tablespoon reduced-calorie mayonnaise
½ teaspoon finely crushed dried tarragon leaves
2 cups chopped cooked turkey breast
½ cup seedless green grapes, halved
4 miniature whole wheat pitas
4 lettuce leaves
1 cup whole strawberries

Combine the yogurt, mayonnaise, and tarragon in a bowl and whisk to blend. Fold in the turkey and grapes. Chill, covered, for at least 1 hour. Trim the tops from the pitas to form pockets. Line the inside of each pita pocket with a lettuce leaf and fill carefully with turkey mixture. Garnish each plate with ¼ cup whole strawberries.

Yield: 4 servings
National Turkey Federation

The same knife should never be used to cut meat and then vegetables, fruits, or other foods—this leads to cross-contamination.

Broiled Lamb Chops and Patties

Thickness	Approximate Total Cooking Time
¾ to 1 inch	12 minutes
1 ½ inches	18 minutes
2 inches	22 minutes

Times shown are for medium doneness. Lamb is not usually served rare.

Beef and lamb should always be cooked to an internal temperature of at least 160 degrees Fahrenheit.

Pesto Pizza

Pesto
1 or 2 unbaked thin whole wheat pizza shells
Slices of grilled free-range chicken
Onions, sliced
Tomatoes, sliced
Green bell peppers, chopped
Fresh mushrooms
Part-skim mozzarella cheese, shredded

Spread a layer of pesto over the pizza crust. Top with slices of grilled chicken, onions, tomatoes, bell peppers, mushrooms, and mozzarella cheese. Bake at 350 degrees until crust is brown at edges and cheese is melted.

Yield: 1 or 2 pizzas

Beef Kabobs

Extra-lean free-range beef

Mushrooms

Green bell peppers

Onions

Tomatoes

Squash

Vinegar and Oil Salad Dressing (page 38)

Cut the beef, mushrooms, bell peppers, onions, tomatoes, and squash into 1-inch cubes and place in a large bowl. Pour 1 recipe of Vinegar and Olive Oil Salad Dressing over the mixture. Marinate, covered, in the refrigerator for 2 to 3 hours. Skewer beef and vegetables and place on a grill rack. Grill over hot coals until done to taste. Cook for about 15 minutes or until beef juices run clear. Turn frequently to avoid overcooking vegetables. Serve on a bed of brown rice.

Free-range cattle have lower fat content in their meat since they exercise by walking and feeding on the open range. Free-range beef does not have the over-abundance of pesticides, antibiotics, or hormones that are usually fed to feed-lot animals.

Curried Lamb

⅓ cup minced onion

¼ cup warm water

3 tablespoons extra virgin olive oil

2 tablespoons coriander

1½ teaspoons cumin

1 tablespoon cardamom

1 teaspoon ground ginger

1 teaspoon turmeric

½ teaspoon garlic powder

¼ teaspoon black pepper

⅛ teaspoon ground red pepper

2 pounds free-range lamb stew meat, cut into 1-inch cubes

2 cups low-sodium beef broth

Celtic salt

¼ cup low-fat plain yogurt

1 teaspoon fresh lemon juice

Freshly cooked whole grain rice

Soak the onion in the water for five minutes; drain. Heat the olive oil in a large skillet over medium-high heat. Sauté the onion in the oil for 5 minutes. Reduce heat to low. Add the coriander, cumin, cardamom, ginger, turmeric, garlic powder, black pepper, and red pepper; sauté for 1 minute. Stir in the lamb and turn heat to medium high. Cook for 10 to 15 minutes or until meat is evenly browned, stirring frequently. Add the beef broth and salt. Reduce heat to medium and simmer, covered, for about 20 minutes or until meat is tender. Uncover the skillet and simmer for 20 minutes longer or until sauce thickens, stirring occasionally. Stir in the yogurt and lemon juice. Serve immediately over the cooked rice.

Yield: 8 servings

Adapted from a recipe found on *MasterCook.com*

Pumpkin Chili

Serve with crackers and hot bread.

3 pounds lean free-range ground beef

2 cups canned pumpkin

2 (10-ounce) cans red kidney beans, rinsed, drained

2 medium onions, chopped

3 (15-ounce) cans diced tomatoes

2 tablespoons chili powder

¼ teaspoon ground red pepper

2 tablespoons sugar (or 12 to 18 drops Stevia)

1 teaspoon salt

2 bay leaves

Brown the ground beef in a skillet, stirring until crumbly; drain. Combine the beef, pumpkin, beans, onions, undrained tomatoes, chili powder, red pepper, sugar, salt, and bay leaves in a large kettle over medium heat. Reduce heat to low and simmer, covered, for 1 to 2 hours, adding water as necessary. Remove bay leaves before serving.

Yield: 12 servings
Adapted from a recipe found on *SeedsofKnowledge.com*

Chicken and Rice Casserole

2 teaspoons extra virgin olive oil

½ red onion, thinly sliced

1 green bell pepper, thinly sliced

2 garlic cloves, sliced paper thin

1 cup water

1 cup uncooked long grain brown rice

4 free-range chicken leg quarters, skinned, fat trimmed

Heat the olive oil in a large skillet over medium heat. Sauté the onion, bell pepper, and garlic in the hot oil for 3 to 4 minutes. Add the water and rice. Arrange the chicken on top. Simmer, covered, for 20 to 25 minutes or until chicken is cooked through, stirring rice occasionally, turning chicken once.

Yield: 3 or 4 servings

Adapted from a recipe found on *SeedsofKnowledge.com*

Bake, grill, or roast chicken rather than cooking it in fat by frying it.

Roast Chicken

1   teaspoon Celtic salt

2   teaspoons fresh thyme, or 1 teaspoon dried

2   teaspoons plus 1 tablespoon extra virgin olive oil

¼   teaspoon plus ½ teaspoon coarse black pepper

8   free-range chicken leg quarters, skinned, fat trimmed

2   pounds potatoes, small or quartered

½   red onion, thinly sliced

4   garlic cloves, minced

1   lemon, quartered

Combine the salt, half the thyme, the 2 teaspoons olive oil, and the ¼ teaspoon pepper in a small bowl; mix well. Rub the chicken with the thyme mixture and place in a large roasting pan. Place the potatoes, onion, garlic, the remaining 1 teaspoon thyme, the 1 tablespoon olive oil, and the remaining ½ teaspoon pepper in a large bowl; toss to combine. Arrange the potato mixture around the chicken. Place lemon quarters on the chicken. Roast at 400 degrees for 1 hour. Check to see if chicken is cooked through, and cook for 15 minutes longer if necessary. Remove lemon. Arrange on a platter and serve.

Yield: 4 to 6 servings
Adapted from a recipe found on *SeedsofKnowledge.com*

Shredded Chicken

The chicken broth may be frozen and later used for soup.

5 to 10 pounds free-range chicken pieces, skinned, fat trimmed

1 to 2 onions, cut up

Garlic to taste

Herbs such as oregano, thyme, sage

Hot peppers such as jalapeño or Thai peppers (optional)

Salt to taste

Barbecue sauce

Place the chicken, onions, garlic, herbs, hot peppers, and salt in a stock-pot over medium heat. Cover with water or chicken broth. Simmer, covered, for about 1 hour or until chicken is "falling off the bone." Drain, reserving the broth for soup. When chicken is cool, take the meat off the bone. Place the chicken in a slow cooker. Stir in your favorite barbecue sauce, enough to make the mixture moist but not soupy. Cook on High for 8 hours, stirring occasionally to break up the meat until meat is shredded. If the mixture looks dry at any time, add more barbecue sauce. Serve with corn bread or on rolls or buns.

Adapted from a recipe found on *SeedsofKnowledge.com*

Beef and Mushroom Stew

Substitute three additional cups of broth for
the burgundy if you like.

3   pounds lean boneless free-range beef, cut into 1-inch cubes

½   cup flour

1½ teaspoons Celtic salt

½   teaspoon black pepper

4   tablespoons extra virgin olive oil

1   large onion, chopped

2   garlic cloves, minced

1   pound mushrooms, quartered

2   (14-ounce) cans low-sodium beef broth

3   cups burgundy

1   pound miniature carrots

2   teaspoons thyme

1   teaspoon rosemary

2   bay leaves

Coat the beef cubes with a mixture of half the flour, 1 teaspoon of the salt, and black pepper, a few cubes at a time. Heat 1 tablespoon of the olive oil in a heavy 5-quart saucepan over medium-high heat. Brown the beef for about 5 minutes, working in batches and adding a small amount of oil when needed. Remove to a platter. Reduce heat to medium. Add the onion to the hot oil, and sauté for about 5 minutes or until tender.

Add the garlic and sauté for 2 minutes. Add the mushrooms and sauté for 5 minutes or just until mushroom liquid is released. Remove the mushroom mixture to a medium bowl with a slotted spoon; cover and set aside. Combine the remaining flour, beef broth, and burgundy in the heavy saucepan over medium heat, whisking until smooth. Return the beef to the saucepan. Add the carrots, thyme, rosemary, and bay leaves. Bring to a boil, scraping up any browned bits from bottom of pan with a wooden spoon. Reduce heat to low. Simmer, covered, for 45 minutes. Remove cover and simmer for 55 minutes longer or until beef is tender; stir in the mushroom mixture for the last 10 minutes of cooking. Discard bay leaves. Stir in the remaining ½ teaspoon salt.

Yield: 6 to 10 servings

Adapted from a recipe found on *SeedsofKnowledge.com*

Oven Beef Stew

Use your favorite steak seasoning for this savory stew.

1   pound uncooked round or chuck steak, cut into thin strips

6   small red potatoes, quartered

½   pound fresh green beans, trimmed

6   carrots, peeled, sliced, or 1 pound miniature carrots

1   small onion, chopped

1   (14-ounce) can low-sodium beef broth

½   cup whole wheat flour

½   teaspoon thyme

¼   teaspoon pepper

2   teaspoons steak seasoning

Combine the steak, potatoes, green beans, carrots, and onion in a 9x13-inch baking dish. Combine the beef broth, flour, thyme, pepper, and steak seasoning in a medium bowl and whisk until smooth. Pour the broth mixture evenly over the steak and vegetables. Bake, tightly covered with foil, at 350 degrees for 40 minutes. Remove foil, stir well, and replace foil. Bake for 20 minutes longer.

Yield: 6 servings

Adapted from a recipe found on *SeedsofKnowledge.com*

South of the Border Stew

1½ cups tomato sauce

½ cup chopped cilantro

2 tablespoons tomato paste

1 tablespoon cumin

4 garlic cloves, crushed

1½ teaspoons oregano

1½ teaspoons Celtic salt

½ teaspoon hot red pepper sauce

12 baby red potatoes, scrubbed, halved

6 medium scallions or green onions, trimmed, sliced

2 pounds butternut squash, halved, seeded, peeled, cut into 1-inch chunks

1 lean free-range beef roast, cut into large cubes

Mix together the tomato sauce, cilantro, tomato paste, cumin, garlic, oregano, 1 teaspoon of the salt, and the hot pepper sauce in a slow cooker. Layer the potatoes, scallions, half the squash, beef, and the remaining squash over the tomato mixture, in the order listed. Cook on Low for 8 hours or High for 5 hours or until beef is tender. Remove the meat and vegetables to a serving platter. Skim the fat from the liquid remaining in the slow cooker; spoon the liquid over the meat and vegetables.

Yield: 4 to 8 servings
Adapted from a recipe found on *SeedsofKnowledge.com*

Western Beef Casserole

1½ pounds lean free-range ground beef

1 garlic clove, minced

¼ cup onion, finely chopped

3 cups canned tomatoes with juice

1 teaspoon Celtic salt

2 teaspoons chili powder

1 teaspoon hot red pepper sauce (optional)

32 ounces dry red beans, cooked, drained

1 cup uncooked brown rice

1 cup freshly shredded part-skim mozzarella cheese

Brown the ground beef with the garlic and onion in a skillet, stirring until crumbly; drain. Chop the tomatoes or process briefly in a blender or food processor. Combine the beef mixture, tomatoes, salt, chili powder, pepper sauce, beans, and rice in a large baking dish. Bake, covered, at 350 degrees for 30 minutes. Uncover, sprinkle with the mozzarella cheese, and bake for 15 minutes longer.

Yield: 8 to 12 servings

Adapted from a recipe found on *SeedsofKnowledge.com*

Tender Slow Cooker Roast

If the roast is too large to fit in your slow cooker, cut it to fit.

1 (3- to 4-pound) free-range beef roast
Celtic salt and pepper to taste
1 pound carrots, quartered
4 or 5 potatoes, peeled, halved
½ onion, chopped
1 tablespoon (about) white or wine vinegar
1 tablespoon fresh thyme, or 1 teaspoon dried

Brown all sides of the roast in a large heavy saucepan, seasoning with salt and pepper. Remove from heat. Pour ½ cup water into a slow cooker. Layer the carrots, potatoes, and onion in the cooker. Place the roast on top of the onion layer. Drizzle the vinegar and sprinkle the thyme over the roast. Cook on High for about 6 hours. Serve with rolls or bread.

Yield: 8 to 12 servings
Adapted from a recipe found on *SeedsofKnowledge.com*

Lamb Stew

**Another way to prepare this stew is to cook it
in a slow cooker on High for about six hours, adding
the mushrooms for the last fifteen minutes of cooking time.**

4 tablespoons extra virgin olive oil

1 garlic clove, halved

½ onion, thinly sliced

3 pounds lean free-range lamb, cut into 1-inch cubes

⅓ cup flour

1½ teaspoons Celtic salt

¼ teaspoon pepper

4 medium carrots, sliced

3 cups low-sodium beef or chicken broth

½ teaspoon thyme

10 to 15 fresh mushrooms, halved

Heat the olive oil in a heavy skillet. Sauté the garlic and onion in the hot oil for 5 minutes; remove garlic and onion to a small bowl. Coat the lamb with a mixture of the flour, salt, and pepper; brown well in the hot oil, adding more oil if necessary. Return the onion and garlic to the skillet. Add the carrots, broth, and thyme. Simmer, covered, for 1½ hours or until tender. Sauté the mushrooms in olive oil for 5 minutes; add to the lamb mixture and mix gently. Simmer for 10 more minutes over very low heat.

Yield: 8 to 10 servings
Adapted from a recipe found on *SeedsofKnowledge.com*

Beef Barbecue

Lean free-range beef roast, cut into 1- to 2-inch cubes
Extra virgin olive oil
Small onion, thinly sliced
Barbecue sauce

Brown the beef on all sides in olive oil in a large skillet over medium-high heat. Remove beef to a slow cooker. Sauté the onion in the remaining hot olive oil for 5 minutes or until soft and slightly browned. Layer the onion over the beef and add enough barbecue sauce to cover. Cook on High for about 4 to 5 hours; then break up the beef chunks with a wooden spoon. Cook for about 2 more hours or until beef is shredded, breaking up beef and adding more sauce or a small amount of water if beef begins to look dry.

Adapted from a recipe found on *SeedsofKnowledge.com*

When eating meat, trim all visible fat from the meat before cooking it. The same goes for poultry fat and skin.

Savory Mustard Thyme Chicken

3   tablespoons coarse mustard

1   tablespoon whole wheat flour

1   tablespoon honey

2   teaspoons cider vinegar or herb vinegar

4   boneless skinless free-range chicken thighs or breasts

⅓   cup bread crumbs

1   teaspoon fresh thyme, or ½ teaspoon dried

¼   teaspoon cayenne pepper

2   tablespoons extra virgin olive oil

Combine the mustard, flour, honey, and vinegar in a small bowl; whisk until smooth. Brush the chicken with the mustard mixture and roll it in a mixture of the bread crumbs, thyme, and cayenne pepper, coating well. Heat the olive oil in a large skillet over medium heat. Cook the chicken in the hot oil, turning once, for about 6 minutes per side, or until well-browned and cooked through.

Yield: 4 servings

Adapted from a recipe found on *SeedsofKnowledge.com*

Marinated Fish

**Grilling time for a fish fillet cooked "medium"
will probably total fifteen to eighteen minutes.**

2   tablespoons chopped fresh parsley

2   tablespoons wine vinegar

2   teaspoons Dijon mustard

1   teaspoon minced fresh thyme, or ½ teaspoon crushed dried

¼   cup minced onion

1   tablespoon extra virgin olive oil

1   clove garlic, minced

1   pound fish fillets

Combine the parsley, vinegar, mustard, thyme, onion, olive oil, and garlic in a large glass bowl; whisk well. Add the fish. Marinate, covered, in the refrigerator for 6 to 10 hours, turning occasionally. Drain the fish, discarding the marinade. Grill over hot coals or broil 3 to 5 inches from the heat source for 15 to 18 minutes, turning once.

Yield: 4 servings

Adapted from a recipe found on *SeedsofKnowledge.com*

Raw fish should be avoided. It is important to cook fish adequately to destroy any parasites that may be in the flesh of the fish.

Rack of Lamb with Honey Hazelnut Crust

1   cup ground hazelnuts
1   cup fresh bread crumbs
3   tablespoons chopped fresh rosemary
3   racks of free-range lamb, trimmed
3   tablespoons Dijon mustard
Celtic salt and pepper to taste
3   tablespoons honey

Combine the hazelnuts, bread crumbs, and rosemary in a small bowl; mix well. Arrange the racks of lamb meat side up on shallow baking sheets. Brush the lamb with mustard and season with salt and pepper. Sprinkle the hazelnut mixture evenly over each rack of lamb. Drizzle with honey. Roast at 425 degrees for 25 minutes or until done to taste. Chill, tightly covered, until ready to serve.

Yield: 3 to 6 servings
Adapted from a recipe found on *Recipezaar.com*

Curried Lamb

1   medium onion, thinly sliced
1   tablespoon whole wheat flour
1   bouillon cube
1   apple, peeled, diced
1 to 2 teaspoons curry powder
Free-range lamb meat, cooked, cubed

Sauté the onion slices in hot oil in a skillet over medium-low heat until yellow. Stir in the flour. Dissolve the bouillon cube in hot water and add to the onion mixture. Stir in the apple. Mix 1 to 2 teaspoons curry powder with a little water and stir into the onion mixture. Simmer, covered, for 15 minutes. Stir in the lamb meat. Cook over medium-low heat just long enough to warm up the meat. Serve with brown rice.

Adapted from a recipe found on *CookbooksOnline.com*

Chicken Barese

The name Barese refers to a region that produces the
finest of olive oils. If you use six lamb chops, fat trimmed,
instead of chicken, the dish becomes Lamb Barese.

3 or 4 potatoes, peeled

1   (3-pound) free-range chicken, cut up

1   (8-ounce) can tomatoes, drained

Garlic and parsley to taste

Celtic salt and freshly ground pepper to taste

½   cup freshly grated Parmesan cheese

3   tablespoons extra virgin olive oil

½   cup water

Cut the potatoes into the shapes of French fries about ¾ inch thick.
Combine the potatoes and chicken in a 9x13-inch baking pan. Break up
the tomatoes and layer over the chicken mixture. Season with garlic,
parsley, salt, and pepper. Sprinkle with Parmesan cheese. Drizzle the olive
oil and water over the top. Bake at 350 degrees for about 1 hour or until
chicken is cooked through and potatoes are tender.

Yield: 4 to 8 servings
Adapted from a recipe found on *CookbooksOnline.com*

Marinated Lamb

**The marinade can be reused. It can be frozen,
or keep it in the refrigerator for about a week.**

1½ cups extra virgin olive oil

¾   cup soy sauce

¼   cup Worcestershire sauce

2   tablespoons dry mustard

⅓   cup fresh lemon juice

1   tablespoon pepper

½   cup wine vinegar

1½ teaspoons chopped parsley

2   minced garlic cloves

1   free-range lamb roast

Combine the olive oil, soy sauce, Worcestershire sauce, mustard, lemon juice, pepper, vinegar, parsley, and garlic in a large glass bowl and whisk well. Add the lamb and marinate, covered, in the refrigerator for at least 2 hours, turning occasionally. Roast at 400 to 425 degrees for 40 to 45 minutes or until the lamb tests done.

Adapted from a recipe found on CookbooksOnline.com

Chicken with Peanut Sauce

Beef or lamb may be used in place of the chicken.

1¼ pounds boneless skinless free-range chicken breasts

2 tablespoons sesame oil

2 tablespoons extra virgin olive oil

¼ cup dry sherry

¼ cup soy sauce

2 tablespoons lemon juice

1½ teaspoons minced garlic

1½ teaspoons minced ginger

¼ teaspoon Celtic salt

¼ teaspoon pepper

Dash of Tabasco sauce

Peanut Sauce

Cut the chicken into ½- x 3-inch strips. Combine the sesame oil, olive oil, sherry, soy sauce, lemon juice, garlic, ginger, salt, pepper, and Tabasco in a large glass bowl and whisk well. Add the chicken; marinate, covered, in the refrigerator for 1 to 12 hours. At serving time, preheat the oven to 375 degrees. Drain the chicken, discarding the marinade. Thread the chicken on wooden picks or small skewers and arrange on baking sheets. Bake for 5 to 10 minutes. Serve with Peanut Sauce.

Yield: 4 or 5 servings

Peanut Sauce

2 teaspoons sesame oil

4 teaspoons extra virgin olive oil

½ cup minced red onion

2 tablespoons minced garlic

1 teaspoon minced fresh gingerroot

1 tablespoon red wine vinegar

1 tablespoon brown sugar

⅓ cup peanut butter

½ teaspoon coriander

3 tablespoons ketchup

3 tablespoons soy sauce

1 tablespoon lemon or lime juice

½ teaspoon pepper

Dash of Tabasco sauce

⅓ to ½ cup hot water

Heat the sesame and olive oils in a small saucepan over medium-low heat. Add the onion, garlic, and gingerroot; sauté for 5 minutes or until softened. Add the vinegar and brown sugar; heat until sugar dissolves, stirring constantly. Stir in the peanut butter. Remove from heat. Stir in the coriander, ketchup, soy sauce, lemon juice, pepper, Tabasco, and hot water. Process in a food processor or blender if a smooth sauce is desired.

Adapted from a recipe found on *CookbooksOnline.com*

Moussaka

1   large eggplant, washed

Extra virgin olive oil

1   pound lean ground free-range lamb

2   medium chopped onions

2   garlic minced cloves

½   cup finely chopped parsley

2   large fresh tomatoes

1   cup water

½   cup white wine

2   tablespoons flour

2   cups skim milk

½   teaspoon Celtic salt

4   large eggs, slightly beaten

1   cup freshly grated Parmesan cheese

¼   teaspoon cinnamon

Cut the unpeeled eggplant into ½-inch-thick slices and place in a bowl with enough water to cover; let stand for about 10 to 20 minutes. Pat dry with a towel and arrange on an oiled baking sheet; brush eggplant slices with olive oil. Bake for 10 minutes; remove from oven. Heat 1 tablespoon olive oil in an iron skillet over medium heat. Add the ground lamb, onions, garlic, parsley, tomatoes, water, and wine; cook for about 6 minutes, stirring frequently. Layer half the eggplant, the lamb mixture, and the remaining eggplant in an oiled baking dish; brush top layer with olive oil. Prepare a sauce by heating 2 tablespoons olive oil in a heavy saucepan over medium-low heat; whisk in the flour and cook for a few minutes, whisking constantly. Slowly stir in the milk and eggs. Cook until thickened and smooth, stirring constantly. Drizzle the sauce evenly over the eggplant; sprinkle evenly with the Parmesan cheese and cinnamon. Bake at 350 degrees for 45 minutes.

Yield: 8 servings

Adapted from a recipe found on *CookbooksOnline.com*

Okra Tomato Beef Skillet

A variation of this recipe substitutes sweet potatoes for the okra.

¼   cup extra virgin olive oil
2   pounds lean free-range beef or free-range lamb, cut in ½-inch pieces
1   medium onion, chopped
1   (6-ounce) can tomato paste
8   medium fresh okra, sliced, or ½ (10-ounce) package frozen okra
Celtic salt and pepper to taste

Heat the olive oil in a large heavy skillet over medium heat. Brown the beef with the onion; drain. Return the beef mixture to the skillet. Dilute the tomato paste with a can of water. Add diluted tomato paste and okra to the beef mixture. Simmer, partially covered, for about 1½ hours or until beef and vegetables are tender. Add water as needed to make a sauce of suitable consistency. Season with salt and pepper. Serve over cooked rice.

Yield: 4 servings

Adapted from a recipe found on *CookbooksOnline.com*

Broiled Salmon Fillets with Fennel Sauce

You can spoon the hot fennel sauce over the salmon at serving time or serve the sauce on the side.

2 pounds boneless salmon fillets

2 tablespoons extra virgin olive oil

1 (¾-pound) head fennel, trimmed

½ cup water

5 tablespoons Olive Oil Butter (see page 3)

⅛ teaspoon nutmeg

⅛ teaspoon cayenne pepper

Inspect the salmon carefully to determine if any bones remain; pull away and discard the bones. Cut the fillets into 4 equal portions, either rectangular or square in shape. Coat the fillets with the olive oil, rubbing on both sides of each fillet. Set aside. Cut the fennel into ¼-inch cubes, making about 1½ cups. Combine the fennel, water, and 1 tablespoon of the Olive Oil Butter in a saucepan over medium-low heat; sauté for 5 minutes.

Combine the fennel mixture and the remaining Olive Oil Butter in the container of a food processor or blender; process to a very fine purée. Broil the salmon fillets 4 inches from the heat source for about 4 minutes on each side. Pour the fennel purée into a small saucepan and bring to a boil. Stir in the nutmeg and cayenne pepper. Simmer, uncovered, for about 3 minutes. Remove the salmon to a warm serving dish. Serve with hot fennel sauce.

Yield: 4 servings

Adapted from a recipe found on *RecipeLand.com*

Broiled Salmon with Lime and Cilantro

½   cup cilantro leaves finely chopped
1   tablespoon extra virgin olive oil
1   garlic clove, minced
½   teaspoon Celtic salt
2   tablespoons fresh lime juice
4   (¾-inch-thick) salmon steaks

Combine the cilantro, olive oil, garlic, salt, and lime juice in a large glass dish and mix well. Remove 2 tablespoons of the marinade and set aside. Add the salmon steaks to the remaining marinade; let stand, covered, in the refrigerator for 10 minutes. Preheat the broiler. Drain the salmon and arrange on a broiling rack that has been sprayed with nonstick cooking spray. Brush with 1 tablespoon of the reserved marinade. Broil 6 inches from the heat source for 3 to 4 minutes. Turn the salmon over and brush with the remaining 1 tablespoon marinade. Broil for 3 more minutes or until fish flakes easily with a fork.

Yield: 4 servings
Adapted from a recipe found on *RecipeLand.com*

A major medical study that involved more than thirteen thousand men in the United States revealed that the risk of dying from a heart attack was approximately 40 percent less for those who ate the most fish.

Lemon Sage Red Snapper

½   cup low-sodium chicken broth

4   (½-inch-thick) red snapper fillets

Celtic salt and pepper to taste

3   tablespoons fresh lime juice

3   tablespoons extra virgin olive oil

¼   teaspoon minced scallion

1   teaspoon crumbled sage

Preheat the oven to 350 degrees. Lightly grease a shallow baking dish large enough to hold the fish in a single layer. Pour the chicken broth in the baking dish. Season the fish on both sides with salt and pepper; place in the baking dish. Drizzle the lime juice and olive oil over the fish. Sprinkle with scallion and sage. Bake for 10 to 12 minutes, basting occasionally with the pan juices.

Yield: 4 servings

Adapted from a recipe found on *RecipeLand.com*

Broiled Fish

Broiling time will be about ten to twelve minutes for a one-inch-thick steak.

Fish steaks

Dijon mustard

White wine

Bread crumbs

Parmesan cheese

Arrange the fish steaks in a greased shallow baking dish; brush fish with mustard. Add enough wine to the dish to reach halfway up the sides of the fish. Sprinkle with bread crumbs and Parmesan cheese. Broil 6 inches from the heat source, turning once, until fish flakes easily with a fork.

Adapted from a recipe found on *CookbooksOnline.com*

Red Snapper with Raisins and Pine Nuts

5   tablespoons extra virgin olive oil
1   (4-pound) pan-dressed red snapper
1   tablespoon rosemary
Celtic salt to taste
¼   teaspoon pepper
1   teaspoon sugar (or 2 to 4 drops Stevia)
¼   cup red wine vinegar
¼   cup water
¼   cup pine nuts
¼   cup raisins

Lightly grease a shallow baking dish with 1 tablespoon of the olive oil. Center the fish in the baking dish; sprinkle with rosemary, salt, and pepper. Combine the sugar, vinegar, and water in a small bowl. Whisk until sugar is dissolved; whisk in the remaining ¼ cup olive oil. Drizzle the vinegar mixture evenly over the fish, and sprinkle with the pine nuts and raisins. Bake, covered, at 400 degrees for 20 minutes. Uncover and bake for 30 minutes longer, basting with the pan juices. Remove from oven. Spoon the raisins, pine nuts, and pan juices over the fish before serving.

Yield: 8 servings
Adapted from a recipe found on *RecipeLand.com*

Red Snapper with Tomato Salsa

1   pound red snapper or other lean fish fillets

Tomato Salsa

1   garlic clove, minced

2   small zucchini, sliced

¼   cup shredded carrots

Arrange the fish fillets in a shallow baking dish. Spread a small amount of Tomato Salsa over the fillets and sprinkle with garlic. Place an equal amount of zucchini and carrots on each fillet. Bake, covered, at 350 degrees for about 10 to 15 minutes or until fish flakes easily with a fork. Serve with remaining Tomato Salsa.

Yield: 3 or 4 servings

Tomato Salsa

1   cup chili sauce

2   teaspoons prepared horseradish

2   teaspoons fresh lime juice

¼   teaspoon Worcestershire sauce

⅛   teaspoon Celtic salt

2   tomatoes, diced

Combine the chili sauce, horseradish, lime juice, Worcestershire sauce, and Celtic salt in a small saucepan over medium heat. Heat until hot, stirring occasionally; do not boil.

Adapted from a recipe found on *RecipeLand.com*

> Most fish have high-quality protein and are a good source of essential nutrients such as zinc, copper, magnesium, B vitamins, and iodine, as well as other minerals.

Leg of Lamb with Yogurt

2½ cups plain yogurt

1   tablespoon Celtic salt

1   tablespoon turmeric

2   tablespoons paprika

¼   cup cumin

½   teaspoon ground cloves

½   teaspoon nutmeg

5   tablespoons extra virgin olive oil

1   (10-pound) leg of free-range lamb, boned, cut into 1-inch cubes

Combine the yogurt, salt, turmeric, paprika, cumin, cloves, nutmeg, and olive oil in a large glass bowl; whisk well. Add the lamb and marinate, covered, in the refrigerator for 8 to 10 hours. Drain; discard the marinade. Skewer the lamb cubes and grill over hot coals for about 7 minutes per side or until done to taste.

Yield: 12 to 16 servings

Adapted from a recipe found on *RecipeLand.com*

Yogurt is high in bone-building calcium. It has been linked to the prevention of colds, allergies, and cancer. It helps lower the LDL (bad) cholesterol levels, fights dangerous intestinal infections, improves bowel function, and blocks ulcers.

Here is what a person will get in a single cup of yogurt:

Calories	*144*
Cholesterol	*14 milligrams*
Carbohydrates	*16 grams*
Fat	*3.5 grams*
Protein	*11.9 grams*
Calcium	*415 milligrams*
Sodium	*159 milligrams*
Potassium	*531 milligrams*

Chicken and Garden Vegetables

1   (3-pound) free-range chicken, cooked, skinned, boned, cut in strips
3   large tomatoes, cut in chunks
1   large green bell pepper, cut in 1-inch slivers
1   cucumber, sliced
4   green onions, sliced
1   (12-ounce) jar marinated artichoke hearts
½   cup black olives, sliced
2   tablespoons red wine vinegar
¼   cup sesame seeds, toasted

Place the still-warm chicken strips in a large mixing bowl. Add the tomatoes, bell pepper, cucumber, and green onions. Drain and chop the artichokes, reserving the marinade. Add the artichokes and olives to the chicken mixture; mix well. Combine the reserved artichoke marinade and vinegar in a small bowl; whisk well. Drizzle the vinegar mixture over the chicken mixture. Refrigerate, covered, until well chilled. At serving time, top with sesame seeds.

Yield: 6 to 8 servings
Adapted from a recipe found on *EatChicken.com*

The foremost guideline for purchasing fresh fish is to make sure the fish is from pure waters. The waters off of Mexico, Argentina, and Chile are extremely pure as are the seas surrounding New Zealand and Iceland.

Roasted Chicken and Vegetables

1 (3½-pound) free-range chicken

1 lemon, sliced

1 medium onion, peeled, quartered

3 sprigs of thyme

Celtic salt and freshly ground black pepper to taste

3 medium leeks, thinly sliced

2 carrots, peeled, thinly sliced

6 red potatoes, quartered

2 turnips or rutabagas, thinly sliced

1½ cups dry white wine

1 (14-ounce) can low-sodium chicken broth

Fill the cavity of the chicken with the lemon, onion, and thyme. Sprinkle the skin of the chicken liberally with salt and pepper. Evenly scatter the leeks, carrots, potatoes, and turnips in the bottom of a large roasting pan. Sprinkle the vegetables with salt and pepper. Place the chicken on top of the vegetables. Pour white wine and chicken broth over the chicken and vegetables. Roast at 425 degrees for 1 hour or until the skin of the chicken is browned, the juices run clear, and a thermometer inserted in the flesh of the thigh registers 180 degrees; stir vegetables and baste chicken occasionally while cooking. Remove the chicken to a cutting board and lift the vegetables into a serving bowl. Pour or ladle the pan juices into a pitcher or gravy boat. Carve the chicken and serve with vegetables and pan juices.

Yield: 4 servings

Adapted from a recipe found on *EatChicken.com*

Lemon Chicken with Capers

4   boneless skinless free-range chicken breasts

⅛   teaspoon Celtic salt

2   tablespoons minced fresh mint

1   tablespoon minced fresh basil

2   teaspoons minced fresh thyme

¼   cup minced sun-dried tomatoes

2   tablespoons extra virgin olive oil

½   cup low-sodium chicken broth

2   tablespoons fresh lemon juice

1   tablespoon dried minced onion

2   teaspoons cornstarch

¼   cup red wine

1   tablespoon small capers

Pound the chicken gently into ¼-inch thickness; sprinkle with Celtic salt. Combine the mint, basil, thyme, and sun-dried tomatoes in a bowl and mix well; spread the mint filling over the chicken. Roll each chicken breast to enclose the filling and secure with wooden picks. Heat the olive oil in a large skillet over medium heat. Brown the chicken in the hot oil for about 10 minutes or until brown on all sides, turning frequently. Stir in the chicken broth, lemon juice, and onion. Simmer, covered, for about 10 minutes or until juices run clear and fork can be inserted in chicken with ease. Remove chicken rolls from skillet; set aside and keep warm. Combine the cornstarch and wine in a small bowl; whisk until smooth. Uncover the skillet. Add the cornstarch mixture to the liquid in the pan and cook, stirring, until mixture is clear and thickened. Stir in the capers. To serve, spread half the sauce in a serving dish; slice the chicken rolls and arrange, overlapping slices, over the sauce layer. Spoon the remaining sauce over the chicken.

Yield: 4 servings
Adapted from a recipe found on *EatChicken.com*

Chicken and Goat Cheese in Grape Leaves

4   boneless skinless free-range chicken breasts
½   teaspoon Celtic salt
¼   teaspoon pepper
6   ounces fresh goat cheese
4   fresh basil leaves
4   fresh sage leaves
8 or 12 grape leaves in brine
1   garlic clove
Sprig of rosemary

Season the chicken with salt and pepper. Spread ¼ of the goat cheese over the top of each piece of chicken. Place 1 basil leaf and 1 sage leaf over each; wrap each with 2 or 3 grape leaves. Place about 1 inch of water in a large saucepan with a steaming rack; arrange the wrapped chicken on the steaming rack. Add garlic and rosemary to the water and bring to a boil. Cook, covered, over high heat for about 20 minutes, making sure the water doesn't evaporate. Serve with potatoes or brown rice.

Yield: 4 servings
Adapted from a recipe found on *EatChicken.com*

Chicken and Mint Relish

4 boneless skinless free-range chicken breasts

2 tablespoons plus 1 teaspoon extra virgin olive oil

1 teaspoon cumin

½ teaspoon sweet paprika

½ teaspoon coriander

¼ teaspoon cinnamon

1½ teaspoons minced fresh gingerroot

1 tablespoon fresh lemon juice

1 tablespoon chopped cilantro

Arrange the chicken in a shallow baking pan. Heat the olive oil in a medium skillet over medium heat. Sauté the cumin, paprika, coriander, cinnamon, and gingerroot in the hot oil for about 1 minute. Remove from heat; stir in the lemon juice and cilantro. Cool slightly and pour over the chicken, turning to coat. Chill, covered, for 20 minutes. Return the chicken to the skillet over medium heat. Cook, turning occasionally, for about 5 minutes on each side, or until a fork can be inserted easily and the juices run clear. Serve topped with Mint Relish and garnished with mint sprigs and lemon slices.

Yield: 4 servings

Mint Relish

1 cup finely diced ripe mango

½ cup finely diced red bell pepper

⅓ cup finely diced red onion

1 tablespoon finely chopped fresh mint

1 jalapeño pepper, seeded, minced

½ teaspoon minced gingerroot

2   tablespoons fresh lemon juice

1   tablespoon extra virgin olive oil

Combine the mango, bell pepper, onion, mint, jalapeño, gingerroot, lemon juice, and olive oil in a small bowl; mix well. Chill, covered, until serving time.

Adapted from a recipe found on *EatChicken.com*

Steamed Fish

The carrots, broccoli, and beans may be partially cooked ahead of time if desired.

2   pounds haddock or other fresh fish fillets

1   cup grated Parmesan cheese

½   cup broccoli florets

½   cup sliced green beans

½   cup thinly sliced carrots

8   slices fresh tomato

½   cup sliced fresh mushrooms

Celtic salt and pepper to taste

Divide fish into 4 portions and place each in the center of a square of aluminum foil. Spoon ¼ of the Parmesan cheese over each portion of fish. Arrange the broccoli, green beans, and carrots around edges of fish; place tomatoes and mushrooms on top. Season. Wrap in foil, sealing to enclose each packet, leaving an air space inside. Place on a baking sheet and bake at 425 degrees for 30 minutes or until vegetables are tender and fish flakes easily with a fork.

Yield: 4 servings
Adapted from a recipe found on *CookbooksOnline.com*

Moroccan Beef with Honey-Spiced Couscous

2 tablespoons red wine vinegar

2 teaspoons minced garlic

1 teaspoon cumin

1 teaspoon coriander

½ teaspoon ginger

½ teaspoon cinnamon

½ teaspoon freshly ground pepper

½ cup honey

½ cup extra virgin olive oil

1½ pounds extra-lean flank steak

Combine the vinegar, garlic, cumin, coriander, ginger, cinnamon, and pepper in a large glass bowl; whisk well. Add the honey and oil; whisk to blend. Remove ⅓ cup of the marinade and set aside, covered, in the refrigerator. Add the flank steak to the marinade in the large glass bowl, turning to coat. Marinate, covered, in the refrigerator for 1 to 10 hours. Drain the steak, discarding the marinade. Heat a little olive oil in a large skillet over medium heat. Brown the steak in the hot oil, about 5 minutes on each side. Reduce heat to low and cook, covered, for 10 minutes for medium doneness. Slice steak diagonally into thin slices. Serve with pan juices and Honey-Spiced Couscous.

Yield: 6 servings

Honey-Spiced Couscous

2 cups water

⅓ cup reserved steak marinade

1 (8-ounce) can garbanzo beans, drained

1   cup chopped fresh tomatoes

⅓   cup chopped fresh parsley

12 ounces couscous

Combine the water, reserved marinade, garbanzo beans, tomatoes, and parsley in a large saucepan over high heat; bring to a boil. Stir in the couscous. Cover and remove from heat. Let stand, covered, for 5 minutes. Fluff with fork and serve.

Adapted from a recipe found on *Honey.com*

Fish consumption has many beneficial properties. It has been shown to:

- *thin the blood.*
- *protect arteries from damage.*
- *inhibit formation of blood clots.*
- *lower LDL (bad) cholesterol.*
- *lower blood pressure.*
- *reduce triglycerides.*
- *reduce risk of strokes and heart attack.*
- *reduce risk of lupus.*
- *fight inflammation.*
- *ease symptoms of rheumatoid arthritis.*
- *help regulate the immune system.*
- *relieve migraine headaches.*
- *soothe bronchial asthma.*
- *combat early kidney disease.*
- *inhibit growth of cancerous tumors in animals.*

Oven-Fried Fish

**Freshwater bass, bluefish, orange roughy, and bluefin tuna
are a few of the fish that can be prepared this way.**

1   pound fish fillets
1½ teaspoons Celtic salt
¼   cup skim milk
½   cup dry bread crumbs
2   tablespoons extra virgin olive oil

If fish fillets are large, cut into serving pieces. Preheat the oven to 500 degrees. Combine the salt and milk in a shallow bowl. Dip the fish into the milk; coat with bread crumbs. Arrange in a shallow 9x13-inch baking dish that has been lightly sprayed with olive oil cooking spray. Drizzle the 2 tablespoons olive oil over the fish. Place the baking dish on an oven rack slightly above the center of the oven. Bake, uncovered, for 10 to 12 minutes or until fish flakes easily with fork.

Yield: 3 or 4 servings
Adapted from a recipe found on *CookbooksOnline.com*

Baked Fish Steaks

Finely chopped parsley, onion, and celery leaves

2   pounds fish steaks

1½ teaspoons curry powder

Celtic salt and pepper to taste

Spread a mixture of the parsley, onion, and celery in a shallow baking dish. Sprinkle both sides of fish with curry powder, salt, and pepper. Arrange the seasoned fish over the parsley mixture. Bake at 350 degrees, uncovered, for 25 to 30 minutes or until fish flakes easily with a fork.

Yield: 4 to 8 servings

Adapted from a recipe found on *CookbooksOnline.com*

VEGETABLES

And you shall eat the herb of the field. (Gen. 3:18)

Vegetables made up a large portion of the foods that Jesus ate. Vegetables add flavor, taste, color, texture, and diversity to each meal, and they are packed with phytonutrients, antioxidants, vitamins, minerals, and enzymes that help prevent cancer, heart disease, strokes, osteoporosis, and most other degenerative diseases.

As you modify your diet to include more vegetables, preserve their nutritional value by eating them either raw, steamed, or lightly stir fried in olive oil. When you can, buy fresh, organic vegetables.

Common vegetables consumed in biblical times included beans, peas, lentils, cucumbers, leeks, and onions. However, there are other vegetables available today that are important for our health. In fact, one of the main dietary recommendations of the American Cancer Society is that people include cruciferous vegetables in their diet to help reduce the risk of cancer. Cruciferous vegetables include broccoli, cauliflower, brussel sprouts, bok choy, collard greens, kale, mustard greens, watercress, turnip greens, radishes, rutabagas, horseradish, and cabbage. These vegetables contain high amounts of phytonutrients that protect us from both cancer and heart disease. However, they are not mentioned in the Bible, probably because they were not commonly available in Mediterranean nations.

Vegetables, especially beans, peas, legumes, and lentils, are high in soluble fiber, which helps lower cholesterol, stabilizes blood sugar, slows digestion, and helps prevent hemorrhoids, varicose veins, constipation, and obesity. Fiber also helps to bind toxins, heavy metals, chemicals, and carcinogens and remove them from the body.

Another important group of vegetables contain carotinoids, found in yellow, orange, and red vegetables, as well as in dark green leafy vegetables. There are over 600 different carotinoids. One of the most popular is beta carotene, which is found primarily in yellow and orange fruits and vegetables, especially carrots. Another important carotinoid is lycopene, which is found in red pigmented foods like tomatoes.

Dark-green leafy vegetables such as spinach, romaine lettuce, kale, collard greens, and parsley, are high in chlorophyll, which is responsible for the green pigment in plants. Generally, the darker green the plant or vegetable, the more chlorophyll it contains. Chlorophyll helps protect our DNA, which is our genetic blueprint, from various toxins, and it has anticancer properties and antioxidant effects.

The key is eating a diversity of colorful, fresh vegetables on a daily basis. If fresh vegetables are not available, frozen ones are an acceptable alternative. And, on occasion, it is acceptable to eat canned vegetables. Try seasoning your vegetables with herbs, spices, grated Parmesan, lemon, or even wine, to enhance their flavor. Serve them as an appetizer, side dish, or main course; in salads; or mixed with pasta or rice.

God's initial plan was for man to be a vegetarian. In the first chapter of the Bible we read, "See I have given you every herb that yields seed which is on the face of all the earth, and every tree whose fruit yields seeds; to you it shall be for food" (Gen. 1:29).

Lebanese Eggplant

1   eggplant, peeled, diced
¼   cup extra virgin olive oil
½   cup onion, chopped
1   garlic clove, minced
½   cup fresh mushrooms, sliced
1   tablespoon whole wheat flour
1   (16-ounce) can tomatoes, drained
½   teaspoon brown sugar
⅛   teaspoon freshly ground pepper
½   teaspoon Celtic salt
¼   teaspoon basil

Cook the eggplant in boiling water in a saucepan for 8 to 10 minutes; drain well. Heat the olive oil in a saucepan over medium heat. Sauté the onion, garlic, and mushrooms in the hot oil for a few minutes. Add the flour, whisking until well blended. Stir in the eggplant, tomatoes, brown sugar, pepper, salt, and basil; bring to a boil. Remove from heat. Spread the eggplant mixture in a 1-quart baking dish that has been lightly sprayed with olive oil cooking spray. Bake at 375 degrees for 25 minutes or until browned and bubbly.

Yield: 4 servings
Adapted from a recipe found on *RecipeSource.com*

Grilled Corn on the Cob

Remove silks and husks from ears of corn. Wash the corn and let it soak in cool water for 15 minutes. Brush grill racks with olive oil. Grill the corn over hot coals for about 15 minutes or until tender, turning frequently.

Mediterranean Stuffed Eggplant

1   eggplant, halved lengthwise
4   tablespoons extra virgin olive oil
½   cup onion, chopped
1   garlic clove, minced
1   (16-ounce) can diced tomatoes, drained, liquid reserved
2   tablespoons whole wheat flour
½   teaspoon oregano or marjoram
¼   teaspoon freshly ground pepper
⅛   teaspoon Celtic salt
½   cup feta cheese or drained cottage cheese

Scoop the pulp from the eggplant, leaving ½-inch shells; chop the pulp and set aside. Place the shells in a microwave-safe dish; microwave on High for 8 minutes or until tender. Heat the olive oil in a skillet over medium heat. Sauté the eggplant pulp, onion, and garlic in the hot oil for 5 to 10 minutes or until tender. Remove from heat. Add enough water to the tomato liquid to make 1 cup and place in a saucepan over medium heat; add the flour and whisk to combine. Cook for 5 minutes or until thickened, whisking frequently. Add the flour mixture and drained tomatoes to the eggplant mixture; mix well. Stir in the oregano, pepper, and salt. Place the eggplant shells cut side up on a baking sheet. Fill with the eggplant mixture. Top with feta cheese. Bake at 350 degrees for 30 minutes or until lightly browned and bubbly.

Yield: 4 servings
Adapted from a recipe found on *RecipeSource.com*

Apple-Filled Acorn Squash

3   acorn squash, halved lengthwise, seeds removed
2   apples, peeled, chopped
½   cup walnuts, chopped
1   tablespoon grated orange zest
½   cup packed brown sugar
2   tablespoons extra virgin olive oil

Place the acorn squash cut side down in a shallow baking dish; bake at 350 degrees for 25 minutes. Combine the apples, walnuts, orange zest, brown sugar, and olive oil in a small bowl; mix well. Turn the squash cut side up and fill with the apple mixture. Bake for 20 minutes longer, or until squash is tender.

Yield: 6 servings
Adapted from a recipe found on *RecipeLand.com*

Apples have been shown to:

- *lower LDL (bad) cholesterol and high blood pressure.*

- *fight viruses.*

- *stabilize blood sugar, an important factor in controlling diabetes.*

- *suppress the appetite without robbing the body of necessary nutrients, which is often of help to those who are attempting to lose weight.*

- *regulate bowel functions.*

- *prevent tooth decay.*

- *help stop the growth of cancer cells.*

Fried Fresh Artichokes

Rinds and juice of 2 lemons

12 fresh artichokes, trimmed

2 tablespoons Celtic salt

1 teaspoon freshly ground pepper

3 cups extra virgin olive oil

Place the lemon juice and rinds in a medium bowl. Add the artichokes and enough water to cover; let stand until ready for use. Drain the artichokes and place, bottoms up, on a cutting board. Sprinkle all over, including between the leaves, with a mixture of the salt and pepper, 1 artichoke at a time. Heat the olive oil in a large skillet over medium heat. Cook as many artichokes at a time as will fit in one layer for 20 to 25 minutes or until well browned. Sprinkle some cold water over the artichokes, several times during the cooking period, in order to produce steam and heat the inside of the leaves. When all artichokes have been cooked, arrange them on a large plate, bottoms down to keep in the moisture. Pick them up at the bottom with a fork and dip them, 1 at a time, in the hot oil again, pressing the leaves to the bottom of the pan. The artichokes will open up like roses and the leaves will become golden and crisp.

Yield: 1 dozen

Adapted from a recipe found on *RecipeLand.com*

Enhancing the Taste of Vegetables

I recently heard about a woman who went to a restaurant on the central coast of California and ordered a green salad. The waiter forgot to bring her dressing on the side, so she began to pick out various greens and nibble them. She was amazed at their taste and exclaimed to her friends, "I'm fifty-two years old, and this is the first time I've tasted lettuce!"

The produce at that particular restaurant was very fresh—the lettuce and other greens had been picked that very morning from farms just about twenty miles away. All her life this woman had eaten produce that was not locally grown, and that had been smothered in heavy salad dressings. She was amazed at the taste of greens she thought she knew well.

Whenever possible, I recommend you eat locally grown, organic produce. A great family activity is a weekly trip to the nearest farmer's market to select fruits and vegetables that may still have some dirt clinging to them, but which are unlikely to have pesticides or waxes added to them.

One of the things that many people discover when they begin to eat the way Jesus ate is that they enjoy the taste of fresh food as never before. The truth is, many people in our nation have grown accustomed to eating foods that are laden with salt, sugar, additives, hydrogenated fats, and other items used in the processing of food. As a nation, we seem to have forgotten what whole, fresh food tastes like.

> *Whenever possible, I recommend that a person eat locally grown organic produce.*

Asian Coleslaw

Serve at room temperature.

1½ tablespoons extra virgin olive oil

3 tablespoons fresh lemon juice

1½ tablespoons balsamic vinegar

½ cup rice vinegar

1½ teaspoons maple syrup

¾ teaspoon Celtic salt

¼ teaspoon freshly ground black pepper

¼ teaspoon cayenne pepper

6 cups thinly sliced red cabbage

¼ cup chopped parsley

3 tablespoons chopped cilantro

¼ cup chopped red onion

Combine the olive oil, lemon juice, vinegars, maple syrup, salt, black pepper, and cayenne pepper in a large bowl; whisk well. Add the cabbage and toss to combine; let stand at room temperature for 1 hour. Taste for seasoning and adjust if necessary. Stir in the parsley, cilantro, and red onion.

Yield: 8 servings

Adapted from a recipe found on *CookbooksOnline.com*

Asparagus with Apple Vinaigrette

1   large apple, peeled, cored, quartered

1   cup water

1   tablespoon honey

¼   cup red wine vinegar

½   garlic clove, minced

1   teaspoon Dijon mustard

1   tablespoon fresh lemon juice

½   cup extra virgin olive oil

Celtic salt and pepper to taste

1½ pounds asparagus, cooked tender-crisp

Combine the apple, water, and honey in a saucepan over medium heat; simmer for about 10 minutes or until apples are tender. Remove from heat and allow to cool. Remove the apple mixture to a food processor or blender and purée. Add the vinegar, garlic, mustard, and lemon juice to the apple purée; process for 1 minute. Add the oil in a fine stream, processing constantly at high speed until smooth. Season with salt and pepper. Arrange the asparagus on individual serving plates and cover each with several spoonfuls of vinaigrette.

Yield: 4 to 6 servings
Adapted from a recipe found on *RecipeLand.com*

Mushroom Wild Rice

4   ounces uncooked wild whole-grain rice

2   cups water

1   tablespoon low-sodium beef bouillon granules

¼   cup extra virgin olive oil

1   tablespoon fresh lemon juice

½   pound fresh mushrooms, sliced

2   tablespoons minced onion

1   tablespoon minced fresh parsley

1   minced garlic clove

½   cup finely chopped pecans

Combine the rice, water, and bouillon granules in a saucepan over high heat; bring to a boil. Reduce heat and simmer, covered, for 30 minutes or until rice is tender and water absorbed. Combine the olive oil, lemon juice, and mushrooms in a skillet over medium heat and sauté for 5 to 10 minutes or until mushrooms are tender. Stir the mushroom mixture, onion, parsley, garlic, and pecans into the rice mixture and serve.

Yield: 4 to 6 servings
Adapted from a recipe found on *RecipeLand.com*

Herbed Baked Potatoes

Substitute 3 teaspoons of dried herbs for the fresh herbs if you like.

4   potatoes
1   teaspoon Celtic salt
3   tablespoons extra virgin olive oil
3   tablespoons chopped fresh herbs such as parsley, thyme, chives
5½ tablespoons freshly grated Parmesan cheese

Scrub the unpeeled potatoes and cut into thin slices, cutting to but not though the bottom. Place potatoes in a baking dish; fan them slightly. Sprinkle with salt and drizzle with olive oil. Sprinkle with herbs. Bake at 350 degrees for 55 minutes. Remove from oven. Sprinkle with the Parmesan cheese; bake for 10 minutes longer until lightly browned, cheese is melted, and potatoes are soft inside.

Yield: 4 servings
Adapted from a recipe found on *SeedsofKnowledge.com*

Just a half cup of raw onion contains the following:

Calories	*27*
Sodium	*2 milligrams*
Potassium	*126 milligrams*
Fiber	*0.6 grams*
Carbohydrates	*5.9 grams*

Onions are also high in vitamins, especially B vitamins such as thiamine and riboflavin, and vitamin C.

Potato Balls

8   large potatoes, peeled
½   cup extra virgin olive oil
Celtic salt
Chopped fresh parsley

Scoop 1-inch balls from the potatoes with a melon ball cutter. Cook the potato balls in boiling salted water for 8 to 10 minutes; drain well. Heat the olive oil in a large skillet over medium heat. Sauté the potatoes in the hot oil until golden brown, stirring frequently to brown evenly. Sprinkle with salt and chopped parsley.

Yield: 8 servings
Adapted from a recipe found on *SeedsofKnowledge.com*

Apricot Couscous

12 ounces couscous
2½ cups water
½   cup dried apricots, sliced
½   cup slivered almonds, lightly toasted
Chopped cilantro to taste
Celtic salt and freshly ground black pepper to taste

Combine the couscous and water in a bowl and let stand for about 30 minutes or until water is absorbed, stirring frequently to keep mixture from becoming sticky. Stir in the apricots, almonds, cilantro, salt, and pepper and place in the top of a double boiler over hot simmering water. Steam for about 20 to 30 minutes. Stir well and serve warm.

Yield: 8 servings

New Potatoes with Peas

Shelling the peas should yield about one cup.

1   pound fresh peas, shelled

2   pounds small new red potatoes

1¼ teaspoons Celtic salt

½   teaspoon basil

⅛   teaspoon pepper

2   teaspoons extra virgin olive oil

¼   cup light sour cream

Minced fresh parsley

Steam or boil the fresh peas just until tender; set aside. Wash and scrub the potatoes, and remove a section of peel from around the middle of each potato. Place in a saucepan over medium heat with water to cover and the salt. Bring to a boil. Reduce heat and simmer, covered, for about 25 minutes or until tender, stirring occasionally. Add the peas and basil about 5 minutes before potatoes are finished; cook until the peas are heated through. Remove from heat and drain. Stir in the pepper, olive oil, and sour cream. Spoon the vegetables into a serving dish and sprinkle with parsley.

Yield: 6 servings

Adapted from a recipe found on *SeedsofKnowledge.com*

Man, from the time of his creation, was an "omnivore," capable of living on both plant and animal foods. Our physical anatomy has been engineered, however, in such a way that we are better suited for consuming more plant products than animal products.

Herbed Potatoes

2   medium or large potatoes, peeled
2   tablespoons extra virgin olive oil
1   small onion, coarsely chopped
1   teaspoon mixed crushed dried herbs
    (thyme, basil, oregano, or rosemary)
2   tablespoons whole wheat flour
1   cup skim milk
1   teaspoon Celtic salt
Freshly ground pepper to taste
Fresh Parmesan cheese, grated

Cut the potatoes into thin 4- to 5-inch-long strips. Place in a saucepan with water to cover; bring to a boil. Reduce heat and simmer for about 15 minutes or until tender; drain. Set aside in a warm dish. Heat the olive oil in a heavy saucepan over medium heat. Brown the onion and herbs in the oil; whisk in the flour. Add the milk, salt, and pepper; whisk well. Reduce heat and cook over extremely low heat, stirring often. Remove the onion with a slotted spoon. Pour the flour mixture evenly over the cooked potatoes. Sprinkle with Parmesan cheese and serve.

Yield: 6 servings
Adapted from a recipe found on *SeedsofKnowledge.com*

Garlic Beans with Dill

If you prefer a garlic flavor that is not quite as strong, remove the garlic clove just before adding the dill.

1   pound green beans, trimmed

1½ tablespoons extra virgin olive oil

6   garlic cloves, peeled, halved

1   tablespoon fresh dill, chopped

¼   teaspoon hot red pepper flakes (optional)

String the green beans and rinse. Cut them into 1-inch lengths and steam for 10 to 15 minutes or until tender; drain. Heat the olive oil in a skillet over very low heat. Sauté the garlic in the hot oil for about 5 minutes or until tender; mash the garlic. Stir in the dill, green beans, and red pepper flakes; cook, covered, over low heat for about 5 minutes. Salt to taste and serve.

Yield: 4 servings

Adapted from a recipe found on *SeedsofKnowledge.com*

Cooking does destroy or reduce some of the allicin in garlic, and it weakens some of the garlic's other theraputic benefits. Whether cooked, raw, or taken in extract form, however, garlic is one of the most potent natural healing foods known to man.

The Health Benefits of Garlic

Garlic has many different health benefits, including a number of benefits to the cardiovascular system.

Japanese scientists have distilled an antibiotic medication called kyolic from raw garlic. Kyolic has also been used to fight influenza—including a severe outbreak in Moscow in the 1950s—as well as to ward off pneumonia, whooping cough, and various intestinal disorders. Researchers are speculating that one of the reasons garlic is such an effective medicine is because it boosts the body's natural immunity.

Studies have shown that garlic appears to help slow blood coagulation, and it has antioxidant properties. It also seems to have mild antihypertensive effects and may lower cholesterol levels. Garlic has been shown to reduce both systolic and diastolic blood pressure. A number of studies have reported that patients using garlic were able to reduce their high blood pressure to manageable levels without using drugs. These anticoagulant, antioxidant, and antihypertensive properties, taken together, make garlic a good ally in preventing atherosclerosis. Only two to three cloves of garlic a day may significantly decrease a person's risk of heart attack.

Baked Tomatoes

8 large tomatoes, halved

Celtic salt

6 garlic cloves, minced

4 tablespoons extra virgin olive oil

1⅓ cups bread crumbs

4 tablespoons fresh basil, chopped

4 tablespoons green onion, chopped

⅔ cup grated fresh Parmesan cheese

Preheat the oven to 425 degrees. Scoop the seeds and juice from the tomato halves and discard. Lightly salt the interior of the tomato shells and arrange on a lightly greased baking pan. Heat the garlic and oil in a small saucepan over medium heat for about 3 minutes. Add the bread crumbs, basil, and green onion, stirring constantly to prevent burning. Fill the tomato shells with the basil mixture and sprinkle with Parmesan cheese. Bake, uncovered, for 15 minutes, watching the tomatoes carefully to ensure they do not become mushy. Serve warm.

Yield: 8 to 10 servings

> *One of the main dietary recommendations of the American Cancer Society is that a person include cruciferous vegetables in the diet to help reduce the risk of cancer.*

Lentils

Lentils were commonly consumed in Israel during biblical times. Lentils are actually one of the oldest cultivated plants. Archaeological evidence indicates that they were cultivated in the Near East as early as 1,800 B.C.

Lentils have 7.5 percent protein, but they are deficient in the amino acids methionine and cysteine. They are very low in fat and contain high amounts of soluble fiber that help to lower cholesterol and control blood sugar.

Lentils are good in combination with other vegetables in soups, stews, and casseroles.

Garbanzo Beans

Another popular bean common to the Middle East is the garbanzo bean, also called the "chickpea." Chickpeas should be soaked overnight in the refrigerator, and the following day, the water should be discarded. I believe chickpeas are best when boiled for about an hour and then ground up in a food processor. To the garbanzo bean mix, tahina, garlic juice, garlic, salt, pepper, and cumin can be added to make what is called "hummus."

Hummus has a cake-batter-like consistency. In Israel, people usually eat hummus by dipping a piece of flat bread (pita bread) into a shallow bowl of the mixture. Olive oil is sometimes added in small quantities. Hummus has been called "the peanut butter of the Middle East."

Chickpeas are also used to make falafel (Middle Eastern meatballs) as well as many other dishes.

Marinated Vegetables

Substitute any favorite vegetables for those that are listed.

¾ cup extra virgin olive oil

1 teaspoon pepper

½ cup red wine vinegar

2 teaspoons dry mustard

2 teaspoons Celtic salt

1 tablespoon oregano leaves

1 head cauliflower, sectioned

6 carrots, sliced

8 ounces mushrooms, sliced

4 ribs celery, sliced

2 red onions, sliced

1 (14-ounce) can artichoke hearts, drained, quartered

1 (9-ounce) jar green olives, drained

1 (6-ounce) can pitted black olives, drained

2 garlic cloves

Combine the olive oil, pepper, vinegar, mustard, salt, and oregano in a large glass dish and whisk well. Add the cauliflower, carrots, mushrooms, celery, onions, artichokes, green olives, black olives, and garlic; mix well. Marinate, covered, in the refrigerator for 24 hours.

Yield: 16 or more servings

Adapted from a recipe found on *CookbooksOnline.com*

Scalloped Corn and Olives

1   (17-ounce) can cream-style corn

1½ cups coarse whole grain bread crumbs

½   cup sliced pitted black olives

1   cup grated Parmesan cheese

2 to 3 cups light cream

1½ teaspoons onion salt

⅛   teaspoon cayenne pepper

1   tablespoon extra virgin olive oil

Preheat the oven to 350 degrees. Combine the corn, bread crumbs, olives, Parmesan cheese, cream, onion salt, and cayenne pepper in a large bowl; mix well. Spoon the corn mixture into a well-greased baking dish; drizzle with olive oil. Bake, uncovered, for 35 minutes or until mixture is set.

Yield: 6 servings

Adapted from a recipe found on *CookbooksOnline.com*

Baked Beets

Wash unpeeled whole beets and remove their tops. Arrange them on a baking sheet and bake at 350 degrees, uncovered, for 1 hour. Let cool slightly. Slip off the skins. Mash the pulp and serve with low-fat sour cream. Squeeze a bit of fresh lime juice over the beets just before serving.

Adapted from a recipe found on RecipeLand.com

Peas and Celery with Olives

2   tablespoons extra virgin olive oil

2   cups sliced celery (cut at an angle in ¼-inch slices)

20 ounces fresh green peas

20 large pitted black olives, halved, drained

½   teaspoon Celtic salt

¼   teaspoon freshly ground pepper

2   tablespoons sliced pimentos

Heat the olive oil in a saucepan over low heat. Cook the celery in the hot oil for 10 minutes, stirring occasionally. Add the peas and cook for 5 minutes or just until peas are tender. Stir in the olives, salt, and pepper. Adjust seasonings to taste. Serve garnished with pimentos.

Yield: 6 to 8 servings

Adapted from a recipe found on *CookbooksOnline.com*

Zucchini Casserole

Slicing the zucchini yields about seven cups.

2   cups small curd creamed cottage cheese

1½ teaspoons basil

1   teaspoon oregano

1   garlic clove, minced

1½ cups pitted black olives, coarsely chopped

2   tablespoons extra virgin olive oil

2   pounds zucchini, diagonally sliced ¼-inch thick

1   medium onion, cut into wedges

½   teaspoon Celtic salt

¼   cup whole wheat flour

2   tablespoons freshly grated Parmesan cheese

Combine the cottage cheese, basil, oregano, garlic, and olives in a bowl; mix well. Heat the olive oil in a heavy skillet over high heat. Sauté the zucchini and onion in the hot oil for about 5 minutes or until tender-crisp. Remove from heat. Sprinkle with the salt and flour; mix well. Layer half the zucchini mixture, the cottage cheese mixture, and the remaining zucchini mixture in a shallow 2-quart baking dish. Sprinkle with Parmesan cheese. Bake, uncovered, at 350 degrees for 30 minutes or until hot and bubbly. Garnish with olives and serve.

Yield: 10 to 12 servings

Adapted from a recipe found on *CookbooksOnline.com*

Zucchini and Carrots with Lemon

4 medium zucchini, washed, trimmed

4 large carrots, washed, trimmed

3 tablespoons extra virgin olive oil

Juice of 2 lemons

2 tablespoons capers

Julienne the zucchini and carrots in strips about 2 inches long. Steam the zucchini for 3 minutes; remove from heat and rinse with cold water. Steam the carrots for 5 minutes; remove from heat and rinse with cold water. Combine the zucchini, carrots, and olive oil in a bowl and toss. Add the lemon juice; sprinkle with capers. Chill, covered, until ready to serve.

Yield: 8 to 10 servings

Adapted from a recipe found on *CookbooksOnline.com*

Baked Mushrooms

2 pounds mushrooms

¼ cup fresh parsley, chopped

1 garlic clove, minced

Celtic salt to taste

1 teaspoon extra virgin olive oil

½ cup whole grain bread crumbs

Fresh Parmesan cheese, grated

Halve the mushrooms; if any are large, cut them in quarters. Spread evenly in a large oiled baking pan. Combine the parsley, garlic, salt, and olive oil in a small bowl; mix well. Dot the mushrooms with the parsley mixture. Bake, uncovered, at 350 degrees for about 30 minutes or until tender and liquid has been absorbed. Before the last five minutes of cooking time, sprinkle the bread crumbs over mushrooms. Sprinkle with Parmesan cheese before serving.

Yield: about 15 servings
Adapted from a recipe found on *CookbooksOnline.com*

Ratatouille

⅓ cup extra virgin olive oil

1 large onion, sliced

2 or more garlic cloves, thinly sliced

2 to 4 zucchini, sliced

1 small eggplant, peeled, cubed

2 green bell peppers, seeded, cut into strips

3 tablespoons whole wheat flour

5 ripe tomatoes, peeled, sliced

Celtic salt and pepper to taste

1 tablespoon capers (optional)

Heat the olive oil in a large skillet over medium-low heat. Sauté the onion and garlic in the hot oil for 5 to 10 minutes or until onion is soft; add the zucchini, eggplant, and bell peppers. Cook over low heat, covered, for about 1 hour, turning gently once in a while so vegetables don't stick to pan. Stir in the flour. Add the tomatoes and simmer, uncovered, until mixture is thick. Season with salt and pepper. Add capers.

Yield: 8 to 12 servings
Adapted from a recipe found on *CookbooksOnline.com*

Marinated Asparagus

½ cup water

½ cup cider vinegar

2 teaspoons chopped parsley

2 teaspoons chopped chives

2 teaspoons chopped pimento

1 teaspoon chervil

1 teaspoon capers

1 teaspoon Celtic salt

⅛ teaspoon pepper

10 ounces asparagus spears, cooked, drained

Lettuce leaves

Blend together the water, vinegar, parsley, chives, pimento, chervil, capers, salt, and pepper. Pour the vinegar mixture over the asparagus. Chill, covered, for about 8 hours; drain. Arrange on lettuce leaves and serve.

Yield: 4 servings

Adapted from a recipe found on *CookbooksOnline.com*

Baked Cucumbers and Onions

2 cucumbers, sliced ¼-inch thick

2 onions, thinly sliced, separated into rings

4 tablespoons whole wheat flour

Celtic salt and pepper to taste

2 tablespoons extra virgin olive oil

Preheat the oven to 350 degrees. Layer the cucumbers and onions in a deep baking dish, sprinkling each layer with flour, salt, and pepper.

Drizzle the olive oil over the top. Bake for about 15 minutes or until onions are tender.

Yield: 4 to 6 servings

Braised Celery and Mushrooms

4   tablespoons extra virgin olive oil
8   ounces sliced fresh mushrooms
⅓   cup hot water
1   low-sodium chicken bouillon cube
4   cups sliced celery
½   cup chopped onion
½   teaspoon Celtic salt
⅛   teaspoon thyme
Pinch of black pepper

Heat 2 tablespoons of the olive oil in a large skillet over medium-low heat. Sauté the mushrooms in the hot oil for 5 to 10 minutes or until golden brown. Remove mushrooms from skillet, and heat the remaining olive oil in the skillet. Add the hot water, bouillon, celery, onion, salt, thyme, and pepper; bring to a boil. Reduce heat and simmer, covered, for 15 minutes or until celery is tender-crisp. Return the mushrooms to the skillet. Heat thoroughly and serve.

Yield: 6 servings
Adapted from a recipe found on *CookbooksOnline.com*

We can eat as Jesus ate by adding more vegetables to our diet, and by eating these fresh, whole vegetables raw, lightly steamed or lightly fried in olive oil.

Baby Potatoes Coated with Almonds

3   pounds new potatoes

¾   cup almonds

2   tablespoons almond oil

2   seeded, minced jalapeño peppers

2   tablespoons grated gingerroot

2   tablespoons minced cilantro

Celtic salt and pepper to taste

Fresh lemon juice

Steam the unpeeled potatoes for about 15 minutes or until tender. Place the almonds in a food processor container and pulse until reduced to a fine powder. Combine the almond powder, jalapeños, ginger, almond oil, and cilantro in a large bowl. Add the steamed potatoes; toss until well coated. Season with salt and pepper and sprinkle with lemon juice. Spear the potatoes with cocktail picks; arrange on a platter. Serve hot.

Yield: 12 to 15 servings
Adapted from a recipe found on *RecipeLand.com*

Braised Carrots, Apples, and Celery

1 teaspoon extra virgin olive oil

3 carrots, peeled, julienned

1 red onion, chopped

3 ribs celery, thinly sliced

2 apples, cored, thinly sliced

2 cups currants

½ cup apple juice

¼ cup apple cider vinegar

¼ cup honey

2 tablespoons Dijon mustard

2 tablespoons fresh basil, chopped

Celtic salt and pepper to taste

Heat the olive oil in a large skillet over medium heat. Cook the carrots, red onion, and celery in the hot oil for about 10 minutes or until the vegetables begin to slightly caramelize and soften in texture. Add the apples, currants, apple juice, vinegar, honey, and mustard. Reduce heat and simmer, covered, for 10 minutes longer. Remove cover and bring to a boil. Boil until the liquid has evaporated and the vegetables begin to glaze. Stir in the basil and season with salt and pepper. Serve warm.

Yield: 4 to 6 servings
Adapted from a recipe found on *RecipeLand.com*

Corn Stuffed Peppers

Three forms of corn are used in this satisfying dish.

4 green or red bell peppers

1 tablespoon extra virgin olive oil

½ cup finely chopped onion

1 crushed garlic clove

½ cup cream-style corn

½ cup corn kernels

½ cup crumbled dry corn bread or tortillas

¼ cup freshly minced parsley

1 tablespoon chili powder

Celtic salt to taste

Freshly cracked pepper to taste

2 cups low-sodium vegetable broth

Fill a medium saucepan at least half full of water and bring to rolling boil. Slice the top from each bell pepper and scrape the insides clean. Plunge the bell pepper shells into the boiling water; parboil for 2 minutes. Remove the bell pepper shells from the water with care. Invert on towels and drain. Heat the olive oil in a skillet over medium heat. Sauté the onion and garlic in the hot oil for 5 minutes or until tender. Cool slightly. Combine the onion mixture, cream-style corn, corn kernels, corn bread crumbs, parsley, chili powder, salt, and pepper in a medium bowl; mix well. Stuff the bell peppers with the corn mixture and arrange in a baking pan. Pour the vegetable broth into the pan around the peppers. Bake, covered, at 325 degrees for 40 minutes, basting occasionally with vegetable broth. Uncover and bake for 10 minutes longer, basting often with vegetable broth.

Yield: 4 servings

Adapted from a recipe found on *RecipeLand.com*

Greek Spinach, Pasta, and Toasted Almonds

**Pasta that is cooked *al dente* is cooked
just enough to be firm, not soft.**

8 ounces mushrooms, cleaned, sliced

16 ounces whole grain ziti or penne, cooked *al dente*, drained

1 tablespoon extra virgin olive oil

5 cups loosely packed fresh spinach, coarsely chopped

2 garlic cloves, minced

1 cup defatted low-sodium vegetable broth

1 (6-ounce) can pitted sliced black olives

½ cup feta cheese

¼ cup toasted sliced almonds

Place the mushrooms in a large heavy skillet that has been placed over medium-high heat and sprayed with olive oil cooking spray. Sauté for 5 minutes or until mushrooms are brown but not mushy. Remove mushrooms from skillet and reserve. Place the pasta and the olive oil in the skillet and toss to combine. Add the spinach, garlic, broth, olives, and mushrooms; toss well. Place on individual plates or a serving platter. Top with the feta cheese and almonds.

Yield: 4 servings

Adapted from a recipe found on *RecipeLand.com*

Curried Mushrooms

Extra virgin olive oil

1   onion, halved, thinly sliced

¼   teaspoon turmeric

2   tomatoes, halved, thinly sliced

8   ounces fresh mushrooms, thinly sliced

Celtic salt to taste

Chili powder to taste

Heat the olive oil in a skillet over medium heat. Sauté the onion and turmeric in the hot oil until onion is tender. Add the tomatoes and sauté for 3 minutes. Add the mushrooms and simmer, covered, for 15 to 20 minutes. Stir in salt and chili powder. Simmer, uncovered, for about 5 minutes or until no liquid remains in pan. Serve hot.

Yield: 4 to 6 servings

Adapted from a recipe found on RecipeLand.com

Gingered Carrots

6   medium carrots, cut into 1-inch pieces

1   tablespoon sugar (or 6 to 9 drops Stevia)

1   teaspoon cornstarch

⅛   teaspoon nutmeg

¼   teaspoon ginger

¼   cup fresh orange juice

Steam the carrots until tender-crisp; drain. Combine the sugar, cornstarch, nutmeg, and ginger in a separate saucepan; whisk in the orange juice. Simmer, covered, until thickened. Uncover, and cook for 1 minute longer, stirring constantly. Remove from heat.

Place the carrots in a serving dish and drizzle with the orange juice mixture, stirring to coat evenly. Let stand, covered, for 4 to 5 minutes before serving.

Yield: 6 servings

Adapted from a recipe found on RecipeLand.com

FRUIT & OTHER

SWEET TREATS

I have come down to deliver them [the Israelites] out of the hand of the Egyptians, and to bring them up from that land to a good and large land, to a land flowing with milk and honey. (Ex. 3:8)

When Americans think of desserts they think of chocolate cake, ice cream, key lime pie, apple pie, or some other form of cake, pie, or cookie. And it has become customary for many Americans to eat some form of sweet dessert at the end of most meals. In fact, the average American consumes about 150 pounds of sugar per year. This equates to over 11,000 pounds of sugar during a person's lifetime, which is about half a truckload.

The types of sweet desserts that Americans commonly consume are eaten very rarely in Mediterranean countries and were eaten especially rarely during the times of Jesus. People in biblical times would eat sweet desserts only at times of feasts, such as weddings and celebrations, and then only in small amounts. Desserts would consist primarily of fruit, occasionally some nuts, and possibly a little honey. Fruit was a main staple in the diet of Jesus.

Americans need to say "no, thank you" to sweet desserts, and "yes" to fruits, nuts and a small amount of honey.

The United States Department of Agriculture has recommended that Americans consume two to four servings of fruit every day. Fruits contain antioxidants, vitamins, minerals, enzymes, and phytonutrients, which help prevent degenerative diseases. In choosing fruits, it's always best to select fresh, organic ones. However, if organic fruit isn't available, simply scrub fruit gently with a mild detergent such as pure castile soap, which is found in most health food stores.

Diversity is also important. Choose an assortment of fruits, including different berries, apples, melons, grapes, and citrus fruits. It is always best to choose the whole fruit instead of the juice, since the juice has a much higher glycemic index, making one more prone to gain weight.

Follow this simple rule: reserve special foods for special occasions.

Honey Cream

¼ to ½ cup honey

2   cups plain yogurt, sour cream, or heavy cream

Place the honey and cream in separate bowls on the table, allowing guests to mix desserts to taste. In winter the yogurt or cream may be served warm; in the summer months, serve chilled.

Yield: 2 to 4 servings
See page 161 of *What Would Jesus Eat?* by Don Colbert

Honey Butter

½ cup (1 stick) butter, melted
¼ cup honey

Blend together the butter and honey. Chill, covered, until serving time. Serve with warm whole grain bread. Use sparingly.

Yield: almost ¾ cup

We do well to eat more fresh, whole fruit daily, and occasionally to treat ourselves to nuts and a little honey mixed into yogurt or drizzled on fruit.

Haroset

**Haroset is a sweet spiced paste that is
traditional at the Passover table.**

¾   cup chopped almonds

¾   cup chopped walnuts

3   cups chopped apples

½   cup raisins

½   cup chopped dates

½   teaspoon cinnamon

¾   cup grape juice or red wine

Combine the almonds, walnuts, apples, raisins, dates, cinnamon, and
grape juice. Serve chilled.

Yield: 8 to 12 servings
See page 163 of *What Would Jesus Eat?* by Don Colbert

Strawberries
and Balsamic Vinegar

Fresh strawberries, washed, hulled, dried

½   cup good-quality balsamic vinegar

1   cup confectioners' sugar

Place the strawberries, vinegar, and sugar in separate bowls. Allow guests
to dip the strawberries into the vinegar and sugar.

Apple Pecan Salad

1   cup chopped fresh apple
1   cup chopped celery
1   cup chopped pecans
1   tablespoon fresh lemon juice
2   tablespoons orange juice
1   tablespoon extra virgin olive oil
1   tablespoon poppy seeds, toasted

Combine the apple, celery, and pecans in a bowl; mix well. Combine the lemon juice, orange juice, olive oil, and poppy seeds in a small bowl; whisk well. Pour over the apple mixture; toss to combine. To prevent apples from turning mushy, serve immediately.

Yield: 4 servings

Fruit Smoothie

If you want to use frozen fruit, first thaw it to room temperature.

10 ounces fresh berries (such as blueberries, raspberries, strawberries)
1   (15-ounce) can peaches or pears
2   tablespoons honey

Combine the berries, undrained peaches, and honey in a blender container; process until smooth. Serve immediately.

Yield: 2 servings

Fruit Torte

**This torte may be used as a dip for your favorite crackers,
or as a topping for bread or muffins.**

8   ounces low-fat cream cheese
Fresh berries
Granola

Divide the cream cheese into even thirds. Soften cream cheese sections individually in the microwave. Spread one section of the softened cheese in the bottom of a well-greased loaf pan. Layer ⅓ of the fresh berries over the cream cheese and sprinkle with ⅓ of the granola. Repeat the cream cheese, berries, and granola layers. Spread a final layer of cream cheese over the second layer of granola. Reserve the remaining berries and granola. Chill the filled loaf pan, covered, for at least one hour or until cream cheese is firm. Loosen the edges of cream cheese with a knife or spatula and invert onto a serving plate. Garnish the top and edges of the torte with the reserved berries and granola. Serve cold.

Yield: 8 servings

Strawberries and Maple Sauce

1   cup low-fat sour cream
¼   cup pure maple syrup
3   pints fresh strawberries, washed, hulled

Combine the sour cream and maple syrup in a bowl and whisk well. Use as a dipping sauce for fresh strawberries.

Yield: 8 to 10 servings

Fruit Salsa

2   apples, peeled, cored, chopped

3   tablespoons fresh lemon juice.

3   kiwifruit, peeled, chopped

8   ounces blueberries

1   pound strawberries, finely chopped

2   tablespoons sugar (or 12 to 13 drops of Stevia)

1 tablespoon brown sugar

Place the apples in a large bowl; toss with lemon juice to prevent them from turning brown. Stir in the kiwifruit, blueberries, strawberries, and sugars. Serve immediately.

Yield: 8 to 10 servings

Fruit Yogurt

1   apple, peeled, chopped

1   orange, peeled, sectioned

½   cup seedless grapes, halved

1   nectarine, pitted, chopped

½   cup strawberries

¼   cup fresh orange juice

Plain low-fat yogurt

Combine the apple, orange, grapes, nectarine, and strawberries in a bowl; mix well. Add the orange juice; toss to combine. Chill, covered, until serving time. Serve with yogurt.

Yield: 4 servings

Peaches and Wine

**Cover the peach mixture and place it in the refrigerator if
you are going to let it stand for more than 1 hour.**

2   ripe peaches, peeled, pitted, sliced
3   tablespoons sugar (or 18 to 27 drops liquid Stevia)
Red wine

Place the peach slices in a bowl. Sprinkle the sugar evenly over the
peaches and let stand for at least 1 hour. Fill wineglasses half full with
drained peach mixture. Drizzle with peach juices. Fill the rest of each
wineglass with red wine. Serve immediately.

Yield: 2 to 4 servings
Adapted from a recipe found on *WhatsCooking.com*

Frozen Banana Salad

1   (6-ounce) can frozen orange juice, partially thawed
1   (10-ounce) package frozen strawberries, partially thawed
1   (20-ounce) can crushed pineapple, drained
6   ripe bananas, mashed
1   cup sugar (or 1 teaspoon Stevia)
1   cup boiling water

Combine the orange juice, strawberries, and pineapple in a large bowl.
Add the bananas slowly, mixing well. Dissolve the sugar in the water;
allow to cool. Pour the sugar mixture evenly over the fruit. Freeze for an
hour or until firm but not hard. Serve immediately.

Yield: 12 to 18 servings

Fruit Coleslaw

1 (8-ounce) can pineapple slices

2 tablespoons lemon juice

1 banana, sliced

3 cups shredded cabbage

1 cup sliced celery

1 (11-ounce) can mandarin oranges, drained

½ cup chopped walnuts

¼ cup raisins

1 cup plain yogurt

½ teaspoon Celtic salt

Drain the pineapple, reserving 2 tablespoons of the juice. Cut the pineapple into small strips. Combine the reserved 2 tablespoons pineapple juice and lemon juice in a large bowl; whisk well. Add the banana and pineapple pieces and toss to combine. Add the cabbage, celery, mandarin oranges, walnuts, and raisins; toss to combine. Blend the yogurt and salt and add to the fruit mixture; stir well. Chill, covered, until serving time. Serve cold.

Yield: 6 to 8 servings

Adapted from a recipe found on *Recipes.com*

Jesus ate a great deal of fruit, some nuts, and some honey.

Melon Shakes

1   cup cubed watermelon
1   cup cubed cantaloupe
1   cup cubed honeydew melon
1   cup low-fat yogurt
2   tablespoons lemon juice
½   teaspoon vanilla extract
½   cup crushed ice

Combine the watermelon, cantaloupe, and honeydew in a blender container; process until smooth. Slowly blend in a mixture of the yogurt, lemon juice, vanilla, and crushed ice; process until smooth. Serve immediately.

Yield: 4 to 6 servings

Grape Honey

4   cups seedless grapes, washed, stems removed
½   cup water

Combine the grapes and water in a small saucepan and bring to a boil. Boil gently for about 20 minutes. Store the mixture in sterilized jars in the refrigerator.

Yield: 1 to 2 cups
See page 148 of *What Would Jesus Eat?* by Don Colbert

Blueberry French Toast

1   loaf whole grain bread, sliced

3   eggs

3   tablespoons sugar (or ¾ teaspoon Stevia)

1   teaspoon vanilla extract

2¼ cups milk

½   cup whole wheat flour

⅓   cup firmly packed brown sugar

½   teaspoon cinnamon

¼   cup Olive Oil Butter (page 3)

1   cup fresh blueberries

Layer the bread slices in a lightly greased 9x13-inch baking dish. Combine the eggs, sugar, vanilla, and milk in a bowl; whisk until smooth. Pour the egg mixture over the bread layer, turning slices to make sure they are well coated. Chill, covered, for 8 to 10 hours. Preheat the oven to 375 degrees. Sprinkle the blueberries evenly over the soaked bread. Combine the flour, brown sugar, and cinnamon in a small bowl. Cut in the Olive Oil Butter until particles are the size of small peas. Layer the flour mixture over the blueberries. Bake, uncovered, for about 40 minutes or until golden brown. Remove from oven. Garnish with additional blueberries and serve.

Yield: 6 to 8 servings
Adapted from a recipe found on *WhatsCooking.com*

Purchase eggs from free-range chickens. Free-range chickens are not given any hormones, antibiotics, or pesticides and they usually feed on grass or grain—all of these factors enhance the nutritional value of the eggs.

Poached Pears with Ginger and Peppercorns

4 cups water

1 tablespoon fresh lemon juice

4 to 6 ripe (not soft) pears with stems

1 bottle dry red wine

1 cup sugar (or 1 teaspoon Stevia)

Juice and grated zest of 1 lemon

4 (½-inch) slices of peeled fresh gingerroot

10 whole peppercorns

Stir together the water and the 1 tablespoon lemon juice in a large bowl. Peel the pears, leaving stems intact, and cut a thin slice from the bottom of each to enable pear to stand upright when served. Place the pears in the lemon water to keep them from browning. Combine the wine and sugar in a pan that is large enough to hold all pears lying on their sides. Bring just to a boil. Add the lemon juice and zest, ginger slices, and peppercorns.

Remove the pears from the lemon water and arrange them on their sides in the wine poaching liquid; add more water as necessary just to cover the pears. Reduce the heat and simmer for 15 to 20 minutes or until pears are tender, turning them occasionally. Be careful not to cook the pears too long or they will turn mushy. Carefully remove the pears to a serving dish. Strain the ginger slices and peppercorns from the poaching liquid. Cook the liquid over high heat until reduced to about ¾ cup and slightly syrupy. Remove from heat. Pour the liquid over the pears. Chill, covered, until ready to serve.

Yield: 4 to 6 servings

Adapted from a recipe found on *WhatsCooking.com*

Blueberry Salad

¼ cup white wine vinegar

1 tablespoon extra virgin olive oil

½ teaspoon sugar (or 1 to 2 drops Stevia)

½ teaspoon Celtic salt

½ teaspoon crushed dried basil

⅛ teaspoon pepper

4 medium potatoes, cooked, sliced

1 cup fresh blueberries

½ cup chopped cucumber

½ cup shredded carrot

2 tablespoons chopped scallions

2 tablespoons chopped parsley

Combine the vinegar, olive oil, sugar, salt, basil, and pepper in a large bowl; mix well. Add the potatoes; mix well. Stir in the blueberries, cucumber, and carrot. Chill, covered, until serving time. Sprinkle with scallions and parsley and serve.

Yield: 10 to 12 servings

Adapted from a recipe found on *FreeRecipes.com*

People who consume the most fruits and vegetables usually have the lowest rates of cancer, hypertension, heart disease, diabetes, and arthritis.

Chilled Strawberry Soup

1½ cups sliced fresh strawberries

¾ cup sour cream

¾ cup heavy cream

2 tablespoons orange juice

2 tablespoons honey

1½ teaspoons finely chopped fresh mint leaves

Fresh strawberry slices, kiwifruit slices, or mint sprigs

Combine the 1½ cups strawberries, sour cream, heavy cream, orange juice, and honey in a blender; process until smooth. Stir in the chopped mint. Taste for sweetness; if necessary, add more honey. Refrigerate, covered, until well chilled. Ladle into chilled soup bowls. Garnish with strawberry slices, kiwifruit slices, or mint sprigs and serve.

Yield: 2 servings
Adapted from a recipe found on WhatsCooking.com

Baklava

1 pound phyllo

1 pound finely chopped walnuts

¾ cup sugar (or ¾ teaspoon Stevia)

1½ teaspoons cinnamon

1½ teaspoons nutmeg

1½ teaspoons ground cloves

2 cups (4 sticks) unsalted butter, melted

Whole cloves

Cover the phyllo sheets with a damp cloth to prevent drying, and allow to thaw for 2 hours. Combine the walnuts, sugar, cinnamon, nutmeg, and the 1½ teaspoons ground cloves in a bowl; mix well. Layer 2 sheets of the phyllo dough in a lightly greased 9x13x2-inch baking pan, brushing each sheet with melted butter, arranging sheets to fit in the pan. Sprinkle 2 tablespoons of the walnut mixture over the phyllo. Repeat the layers of phyllo, butter, and walnut mixture until all phyllo dough is used, finishing with a double layer of phyllo and butter. Chill for 15 to 20 minutes to allow butter to set. Remove from refrigerator and cut dough into diamond shapes with a sharp knife. Pierce each diamond with a whole clove. Bake at 350 degrees for 45 to 60 minutes or until golden brown. Remove from oven and drizzle immediately with warm Honey Syrup. Allow to cool completely at room temperature. Place each diamond in a muffin paper and serve.

Yield: 2 to 3 dozen

Honey Syrup

2   cups water
¾   cup sugar (or ¾ teaspoon Stevia)
1   cup honey

Combine the water, sugar, and honey in a saucepan over high heat; bring to a boil. Boil for 10 minutes. Cool slightly before pouring over hot pastry.

Adapted from a recipe found on CookbooksOnline.com

APPENDIX:

COOKING TIPS

Each of us must take a new look at why we choose to eat what we eat. Rather than continue our mindless, unconscious habits, we need to be intentional and rational about what we choose to put into our bodies. We need to take a serious look at the bad habits into which we have fallen and choose to make a change when we find ourselves in error.

Equivalent Measures

3 teaspoons = 1 tablespoon

4 tablespoons = ¼ cup

5 tablespoons + 1 teaspoon = ⅓ cup

8 tablespoons = ½ cup

12 tablespoons = ¾ cup

16 tablespoons = 1 cup (8 fl. oz)

2 cups (1 pint) = 16 fl. oz

4 cups (2 pints) = 1 quart (32 fl. oz)

8 cups (4 pints) = ½ gallon (64 fl. oz.)

4 quarts = 1 gallon (128 fl. oz.)

Freezing Tips

- Place a sheet of freezer paper or waxed paper in between pieces of meat in order to easily remove only the portions to be cooked.

- Some foods do not freeze well. Those to be avoided are:
    cooked egg whites
    salad greens
    raw tomatoes
    apples
    grapes

- When cooking meat, pasta, vegetables, and casseroles for freezing, slightly undercook items to prevent overcooking when the items are reheated. Add some seasonings when you reheat. Some spices, such as freshly ground pepper, tend to become bitter in the freezer.

- When thawing sauces and gravies they may appear lumpy, but thawing slowly and stirring constantly can usually remove the lumps. Frozen gravies or sauces may be a bit thicker in consistency after they are thawed. Add a bit of appropriate liquid—milk, broth, wine, or bouillon—to thin the sauce to the desired consistency.

- To preserve fresh herbs in the freezer, rinse and dry thoroughly. Wrap in aluminum foil or place in a freezer bag. Place this package inside an airtight, freezer-safe plastic container or a glass jar. Freeze immediately.

- To ripen green pears, place two or three in a paper bag. Roll the top down loosely and store at room temperature out of direct light.

- Add a tablespoon of olive oil to the water when cooking rice, dried beans, and pasta to prevent boiling over. Always run cold water over pasta to remove excess starch. Reheat over hot water.

- If a soup tastes overly salty, place a raw piece of potato in the pot to absorb the salt.

- To remove fish odor from kitchen utensils rinse in a solution of one teaspoon baking powder to one quart water. Rubbing a fresh lemon over your hands is an easy way to remove fish and onion odors.

- Never soak vegetables after slicing or you will lose many of the nutrients in the water.

Volume of Baking Pans

When the recipe calls for . . .

4-cup baking dish, use:

9" pie plate
8 x 1¼" layer cake pan
7⅛ x 3⅝ x ¼" loaf pan

6-cup baking dish, use

8 or 9 x 1½" layer cake pan
10" pie plate
3⅝ x 8½ x 2⅝" loaf pan

8-cup baking dish, use:

8 x 8 x 2" square baking pan
7 x 11 x 1½" baking pan
5 x 9 x 3" loaf pan

10-cup baking dish, use:

9 x 9 x 2" square pan
7½ x 11 x 1½?" baking pan
10 x 15 x 1" jelly roll pan

12-cup baking dish, use:

8½ x 13½ x 2" glass baking pan

15-cup baking dish, use:

9 x 13 x 2" metal baking pan

19-cup baking dish, use:

10½ x 14 x 2½" roasting pan

Emergency Ingredient Substitutions

It is always best to use the ingredients recommended in a recipe. Substitutions should only be used in rare instances, as recipe results can vary.

FOR	USE
Baking powder, 1 teaspoon	½ teaspoon cream of tartar plus ¼ teaspoon baking soda
Cornstarch, 1 tablespoon	2 tablespoons all-purpose flour or 2 teaspoons tapioca
Flour, 1 cup all-purpose	1 cup plus 2 tablespoons cake flour
Flour, 1 cup self-rising	1 cup all-purpose flour plus 1½ teaspoons baking powder and ½ teaspoon salt
Buttermilk, 1 cup	1 tablespoon lemon juice or white vinegar plus enough milk to make 1 cup; let stand a few minutes (or use 1 cup plain yogurt)
Low-fat milk, 1 cup	½ cup evaporated milk plus ½ cup water (or use nonfat dry milk prepared as directed on package)
Fresh herbs, 1 tablespoon	1 teaspoon dried herbs
Fresh onion, 1 small	1 tablespoon instant minced onion, rehydrated
Tomato juice, 1 cup	½ cup tomato sauce plus ½ cup water
Honey, 1 cup	1 to 1¼ cups sugar plus ¼ cup liquid

Setting up the Ideal Pantry

The ideal pantry should include these general food items:

- *Bread.* Select whole-grain breads or whole-grain pita bread. If you are allergic to wheat, choose millet bread or brown rice bread (available at most health food stores).

- *Cereal.* Choose GoLean soy cereal, All Bran, Fiber One, Shredded Wheat, Grape Nuts, natural granola (without any sugar added), old-fashioned oatmeal (not instant), or Oat Bran. If you are allergic to wheat, try millet cereal or any gluten-free whole-grain cereal.

- *Cheese.* Choose Parmesan (freshly grated, or in a block you can grate yourself), part-skim mozzarella, or feta cheese. If you are sensitive or allergic to dairy products, choose soy cheese. I recommend organic cheeses.

- *Eggs.* Choose free-range eggs.

- *Fish.* Choose fish with scales and fins. Avoid catfish and shellfish. Make sure the fish is fresh and from unpolluted waters.

- *Fruit.* Fresh is best. Frozen is acceptable. Avoid canned fruit packed in syrup.

- *Herbs and Spices.* Many Mediterranean recipes call for garlic powder, parsley, Celtic salt (available in most health food stores), and black pepper. Experiment with herbs and spices—they are a great way to add flavor to your cooking without adding fat or sugar.

- *Meat*. Choose free-range meat. Avoid pork.

- *Milk*. Choose skim milk and skim milk yogurt or cottage cheese. Soy milk, rice milk, and almond milk are good choices if a person is sensitive or allergic to dairy products.

- *Nuts*. Almonds and walnuts are preferred. Keep nuts sealed in bags after they are opened and store them in the refrigerator or freezer.

- *Olive oil*. Choose extra virgin or virgin olive oil.

- *Pasta*. Choose whole-grain pasta products. If you are allergic to wheat, try spelt or rice pasta.

- *Poultry*. Choose free-range chicken or turkey, preferably white meat portions.

- *Soups and Broths*. Choose low-sodium, low-fat natural broths (available at most health food stores) that are low in food additives.

- *Starches*. In addition to pasta, choose brown rice or wild rice, beans, legumes, lentils, coarse cornmeal or polenta, and potatoes (fresh, never instant).

- *Sweets*. Stock a little honey. Consider using Stevia (a natural food source that is very sweet and can be readily added to foods instead of artificial sweetener). It is good for diabetics and has no harmful side effects. You may also want to have a little naturally sweetened (no sugar added) fruit spread.

- *Vegetables*. Choose fresh or frozen. Low-sodium canned vegetables are acceptable on occasion. These vegetables are especially good: asparagus, broccoli, cabbage, carrots, peppers, olives, onions, spinach, tomatoes, Brussels sprouts, cauliflower, collard greens, kale, squash, turnip greens, and zucchini. Choose dark green lettuce such as romaine over iceberg lettuce, which does not have nearly as many nutrients.

- *Vinegar*. Choose balsamic, red wine, or apple cider vinegar.

- *Wine*. Choose red.

- *Yogurt*. Choose plain, skim, or low-fat.

Always remember—what you bring home from the store is what you have available to eat. If you don't bring junk food home, you won't eat junk food at home.

Stevia Information and Conversion Chart

Wherever we've listed sugar as an ingredient, we have also listed the approximate Stevia conversion amount. You will find that as you use Stevia more and more, you'll discover the amount that tastes "just right" to you. As when using any sweetener, the amount preferred will vary depending on the person doing the tasting.

There are several different companies that produce Stevia, and the quality can vary. Some companies offer the pure Stevia powder with a filler, which dilutes the sweetness. Others provide the pure powder form, which is strongest. We have found that for cooking, the liquid concentrate form seems to work best. It's easy to measure out in small quantities, and many people use this form to sweeten their tea or coffee.

We've provided a chart that will give you the approximate conversion amounts from sugar to Stevia in the powder and liquid forms.

Sugar	Stevia powder	Stevia liquid
1 cup	1 teaspoon	1 teaspoon
1 tablespoon	1/4 teaspoon	6 to 9 drops
1 teaspoon	a pinch	2 to 4 drops

INDEX

INDEX

INDEX

INDEX

INDEX

ABOUT THE AUTHOR

Don Colbert, M.D., a family practitioner since 1987, is the author of such bestsellers as *Walking in Divine Health*, The Bible Cure Booklet Series, and *What You Don't Know May Be Killing You*. He writes monthly columns for *Charisma* magazine and Joyce Meyers's *Partners* magazine. Dr. Colbert developed his own vitamin line, Divine Health Nutritional Products, and hosts a national talk show entitled *Your Health Matters* with his wife, Mary. He regularly speaks at national seminars on such topics as "Living in Divine Health" and "The Seven Pillars of Health." He makes his home in the Orlando, Florida area.

You may contact Dr. Colbert at:

www.drcolbert.com

or

(407)331-7007

The Christian market is flooded with diet and exercise programs, each claiming to be "God's way" to healthy living. While some of them are based on biblical principles, and some have even proven effective for weight loss, there is not one program leading the pack daring to answer the question *What Would Jesus Do?* Or better yet, *What Would Jesus Eat?*

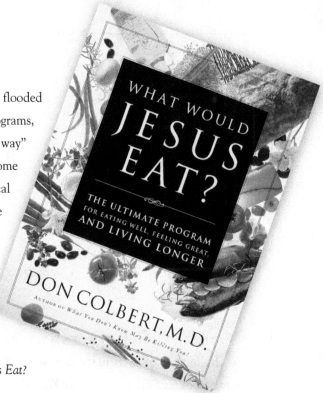

This comprehensive eating plan examines Scripture and reveals what we *know* Jesus ate and what we can confidently infer He ate. Using current medical research, *What Would Jesus Eat?* demonstrates why the diet Jesus followed is ideal for twenty-first century living as well. Readers will:

- Understand why foods forbidden in the Old Testament dietary laws are unhealthy for us.
- Learn how to follow Jesus' eating model with foods that are available today
- Realize the health benefits of the food Jesus ate and the health risks of the food He avoided.

The second half of the book equips the reader with tools to effectively follow the plan — recipes, nutritional information, and practical advice.

For those desiring to safely lose weight and for those seeking a healthier, Bible-based eating program, the only question to ask is, *What Would Jesus Eat?*

ISBN: 0-7852-6567-8

I f you haven't met my best friend, Jesus, I would like to take this opportunity to introduce Him to you. It is very simple.

If you are ready to let Him come into your heart and become your best friend, just bow your head and sincerely pray this prayer from your heart:

Lord Jesus, I want to know You as my Savior and Lord. I believe You are the Son of God, and that You died for my sins. I also believe You were raised from the dead and now sit at the right hand of the Father praying for me. I ask You to forgive me for my sins and change my heart so that I can be Your child and live with You eternally. Thank You for Your peace. Help me to walk with You so that I can begin to know You as my best friend and my Lord.

Amen

If you have prayed this prayer, we rejoice with you in your decision and your new relationship with Jesus. Please contact a local church in your area and attend regularly. Begin reading the Bible daily, starting with the book of Matthew.

Printed in the USA
CPSIA information can be obtained
at www.ICGtesting.com
JSHW012122070124
54776JS00012B/5